WANNA PEEK INTO MY NOTEBOOK?

Notes on Pinay Liminality

"What I admire most in Barbara Jane Reyes' writing is her insistent, critical inquiry into the nature of the Pinay experience and writing. *Wanna Peek into My Notebook? Notes on Pinay Liminality* invites you into the author's process, her willingness to "write through the ugliness and horror," to examine and disrupt perceived notions about Pinays and WOC—whether in family, society, world literature, even in language itself. We learn about the contexts and history, the influence of family and community on her poetry. Reyes' literary explorations have always ventured along multiple routes, yet she has developed a consistent path of questioning that becomes the writing itself— which, by the way, is not always in the form of poems, but also blog posts, memes, spoken word, journal excerpts, and essays. One somehow becomes a participant in her journey—one of struggle and joy, and complexity. This process has created a significant body of multifaceted work addressing the times, lives, and struggles of Pinays in the diaspora. Reyes' notes and prose in Wanna Peek, as well as her poems, return me to the kitchens, dance halls, bedrooms, offices, and classrooms of my youth—where I find that, inspired by her passion and perseverance, I still have questions to ask, things to figure out." — **Jean Vengua**, author of *Marcelina*

"These critical and East Bay tender third world feminist lyrics model for us what it means to commit to the unglorified "work of arriving," to care rigorously about craft, and to craft religiously a genuine care for community. Poet-teacher-kasama Barbara Jane Reyes defetishizes the creative politics of poetic life. Through a decade's worth of intimate autohistoria-teoría, Reyes documents the interiority of her previous books, chronicles the day of her father's passing, humbly mourns and uplifts mentors such as our beloved Al Robles, insistently questions who gets to tell the Pinay's story, invites us into a deep genealogy of Pinay literature, and manifests a feminist poetics of dailiness, revision, rethinking, and reckoning. A memoir, a bridge, a lyric, a liminality, this book is a gift from that cool rebellious poet friend who never stops reading, learning, writing, reflecting, and sharing, who sees in us our multitudes, and wants for us nothing short of pure self-determination and possibility." — **Jason Magabo Perez**, author of *this is for the mosTless*

"The passion and prolificacy of Barbara Jane Reyes blooms from, to crib Prof. N.V.M. Gonzalez, the "rhizomatous nature" of the Filipino voice. She is a chronicler whose words bear the watermark of their own specific place and time, while her imagination stretches across history, heritage, and memory. As history is reflective, she evokes our own passage(s) through time, how ways of seeing inform ways of living. If heritage is the sum of cultural treasures, we find memories of our own families and personal moments in the nuances, chemistry, and music of her language. As interstellar black holes bend time and light, she demonstrates how poets, as forces of gravity, bend or re-make the "rules" of language. Her unstoppable catalogue is a defiance against silence and marginalization, while a compassionate light for others, most especially Filipinos of the world who, beyond place and time, grow from a common root: an identity undeniably our own, which we're all responsible for nourishing." — **Allan G. Aquino**, poet and professor of Asian American Studies at California State University, Northridge

"Those of us who have caught on early to Barbara Jane Reyes have been fortunate to follow her slow, strong, and steady evolution coupled with a rhyming evolution within culture and society, every step of the way. Those just tuning in, you're at the threshold of giant steps. If I may cross a "t" to that – for the past five or so decades, I've been silently but keenly following the unfolding of one of the great open secrets of our times: voices in general society hithertofore underground or too unheard now becoming known and coming into their own. Within that broad perspective, IMHO, Barbara Jane Reyes is a vital ark sailing forwards on the tidal surge of our human ancestors and descents. My life and work is ennobled by her presence and power in our midst, all ways." — **Gary Gach**, author of *Pause Breathe Smile – Awakening Mindfulness When Meditation Is Not Enough*

BARBARA JANE REYES

Wanna Peek Into My Notebook?

Notes on Pinay Liminality

Paloma Press
2022

ISBN: 9781734496581

Library of Congress Control Number: 2021937400

Cover Art: Mel Vera Cruz

Book Design: C. Sophia Ibardaloza

PALOMA PRESS
San Mateo & Morgan Hill, California
Publishing Poetry + Prose since 2016
www.palomapress.net

Table of Contents

Is this Diasporic Pinay Mythopoetics?

I would like to begin to learn how to see into the underside of the world. I need to understand the symbols of my forebears' language of daily struggle.
— Marjorie Evasco, "The Other Voice: Reply to Anzaldúa"

Dear Christina,

Thank you for reaching out to me about writing Filipino cultures and mythologies. You are so right, that being Filipino in diaspora is fraught; we hang on to the sparest threads we can find and recover from confusing childhood memories. I see how intense we become, how fiercely protective of a thing we barely understand, that we've grown up so disconnected from, these talk story inheritances which we oftentimes believe is all we have left of our elders, and our distant memories of a distant "home" that is not our home. My homeland ceased being the Philippines a long time ago, and my stories come from elders also subtracted from that homeland, educated in colonial systems, pushing themselves through decades of toxic American workaholic culture.

You ask where I began with Philippine mythologies. When I was very young, my mother's mother, who was from Baguio, came to live with us in our suburban tract home in Fremont, the first home my parents ever bought in this country, when they were only in their 20s. She told me the story of a god who shaped people out of clay, and baked them in an earthen oven. The ones baked just right were us.

Decades later in Robert Black's Native American History class at UC Berkeley, I read the Pima story of the "Well-Baked Man," in Erdoes and Ortiz's *American Indian Myths and Legends*. Its narrative was almost exactly the same as my grandmother's, which I later found out, through reading Damiana Eugenio's *Philippine Folk Literature: The Myths (Philippine Folk Literature Series #2)*, was the Ifugao story of Kabunian, who created human beings out of clay. We were the "sturdy and perfectly moulded form of a little brown fellow." Sturdy. Perfect.

When I was at UP Diliman in the 1990s, I picked up the anthology, *Forbidden Fruit: Women Write the Erotic*. Two pieces that stood out for me were Maria Elena Paterno's "A Song in the Wind," spoken (sung?) from the point of view of a mermaid, rejecting the conventional myths of her; and Noelle Quinto de Jesus's "Equivalents," in which a pregnant Filipina, raised on aswang narratives, finds terror, pleasure, and power in her dreams and in her own body.

What I remember of my first reading of Paterno's story was that her mermaid's voice was forceful, gorgeous, speaking of her own desire versus being the object of a man's desire — a rejection of man's tongue in favor of her own, nothing I had previously encountered. I also learned about some sea deities in Sylvia Tiwon's Southeast Asian Studies classes at UC Berkeley, and this was common sense; island nations locating power in (bodies of) water. But when I started Google searching mermaids and the Philippines, I found mostly Christianized narratives of dutiful daughters and peasants gifted with daughters as a reward for their hard work and sacrifice. I wanted something wilder, dangerous as seas are dangerous and frightening and wild.

Since reading Paternos, there have been mermaids inhabiting my poetry; with Paternos's work in mind, I wrote my first mermaid poem, "Sirena (The Mermaid) Sings," in the 1990s. It was published in *Babaylan: An Anthology of Filipina and Filipina American Writers*, edited by Nick Carbó and Eileen Tabios. A mermaid has lived in my books, and so did/do other mythic presences.

Filmmaker Matthew Abaya once told me of an idea he had, about a mermaid stuck in the San Francisco sewer systems, which inspired me to write some specific poems, "[objet d'art: exhibition of beauty in art loft victorian claw tub]," and "[the siren's story]," as well as "[evidence]," a poem trying to debunk her as a tourism gimmick, that became part of *Poeta en San Francisco*.

When I was writing *Diwata*, I asked the folks in my grandfather's town of Gattaran, situated on the Cagayan River, about that river's mermaid, about which my titas used to warn us. The folks definitely got tired of me, the annoying American who didn't know how to read the room and just shut up. In my persistence, I witnessed some of these folks go from categorical denial of her existence, to "there's no more mermaid here," which then changed my line of questioning to, "where did she go," "when did she go," "why did she go," and so on.

My interest in aswang and manananggal came later, after meeting and talking with Rachelle Cruz, who was writing the book that became

God's Will for Monsters, and I always remember de Jesus's story, as well as Lynda Barry's "Aswang," a powerful and frightening, unknowable presence in *One! Hundred! Demons!* I also remember Peque Gallaga's film, *Aswang* (1992), which my family and I rented on VHS and watched with glee and horror, but mostly glee. My interest in the aswang and manananggal became about breaking and repairing oneself, the wildness and monstrosity of girls and women finding their own power, acting outside of social boundaries, and embracing all that is not conventionally, socially beautiful, thus falling outside of patriarchal gendered demands. I am fiercely proud of being a monstrous, transgressive, diasporic Filipina. How powerful these Filipina voices were. How could this not appeal to me.

~

Before the internet, my "field" was Arkipelago Books, the card catalog in the Southeast Asian Studies Library at UC Berkeley and my Southeast Asian Studies professors, pilgrimages to the small Filipiniana sections of bookstores in Metro Manila, and oral tradition if elders were properly requested (and lubricated with offerings of Tanduay Rhum and Fundador brandy) to tell.

When my parents saw my interest in Philippine mythologies, and Philippine Studies, they were surprised, precisely because they raised us here, to be successful, proper English-speaking Americans. They did not discourage me though. Others in my extended family see my interest in Philippine mythologies as inextricable from my life as a writer and educator in Philippine Studies: Storytelling. Worldbuilding. I don't know what the "average Filipino" thought, or thinks now about these mythology-inspired books and art. I do know that mythology is powerful, full of potent symbols, and full of other worldviews and cultures many of us feel we have been deprived of as Americans.

You ask why the vast, rich world of Philippine mythologies (which is bigger than some better known mythologies), has had such a hard time finding appreciation, at home and globally. I think this is true for the same reason that Filipino narratives can be "underappreciated" — many diasporic Filipinos cannot find access to the works of artists, writers, creators, typically subsumed and drowned in mainstream-defined, easily consumable "Asian American" or multicultural literatures and arts; because our works exist in spaces alternative or counter to mainstream and popular cultures; because we have been taught that our success as diasporic Filipinos is achieved when we direct ourselves outward and towards whiteness and whitewashed narratives, away from our own.

I wonder also, given Western-centric beliefs about success, whether "pre-colonial" beliefs and narratives are dismissed as an undesirable darkness, as backwards superstition, therefore not worthy of serious study, art, or high culture. These are just questions, and not accusations.

ᵘᶜ

Some of my reading, viewing, sharing and kuwento making:

Damiana L. Eugenio, *Philippine Folk Literature: The Myths (Philippine Folk Literature Series #2)* (University of the Philippines Press, 1993), which I originally bought in a campus bookstore at UP Diliman. I later found other books in this series at Arkipelago Books.

I recently picked up Frank Lynch and Gilda Cordero-Fernando, *The Aswang Inquiry* (Anvil Publishing, 1998). I think I also found this at Arkipelago, if not in a National Bookstore somewhere in Metro Manila. I was already familiar with Cordero-Fernando's output as a fiction writer, and then as a prolific producer of books on Philippine cultures.

Another book I picked up when I was at UP Diliman is Merlinda Bobis's *Cantata of the Warrior Woman, Daragang Magayon: An Epic* (Babaylan Women's Pub. Collective, Institute of Women's Studies, St. Scholastica's College, 1993), a bilingual long poem, a verse reimagining the story of Maria Makiling, not as a forlorn helpless maiden but as a warrior woman who fought and died with and for her people. Bobis wrote this epic poem as a one-woman performance, and it is only now that I am starting to understand how important and paradigm-shifting Bobis's work is.

Jordan Clark's *The Aswang Phenomenon* (2011) is a documentary I found online just Google searching "aswang" a long time ago, and which I found comprehensive and helpful. The narrator's North American outsider point of view, and the fact that Peque Gallaga was one of the interviewees, were some of the more interesting pieces for me. I am an outsider to Philippine cultures and mythologies. I did not grow up with the "correct" or insider language, knowledge, or extensive life experience, just a couple of stories my grandmother told me in Fremont, when I was very young.

These days, my sources for Philippine mythologies are contemporary Filipino authors of speculative fiction, such as Dean Francis Alfar — my intro to Alfar's work was *The Kite of Stars* (Anvil Publishing, 2007) — and now, Isabel Yap's *Never Have I Ever* (Small Beers Press, 2021),

Arnold Arre's phenomenal *The Mythology Class* (1999), and Budjette Tan's wildly popular *Trese*, for carrying these narratives into contemporary literary and popular culture worlds. Alfar's and Arre's books I bought in the Philippines (Powerbooks in Shangri-La Plaza, if I remember correctly). Yap and Tan are widely available, which I love, because readers far and wide witness the centering of young Filipino women coming into their power.

My sources also include fellow Filipino American writers and artists conducting their own research or creating from their own oral traditions, such folks as author Rachelle Cruz, horror filmmaker Matthew Abaya, and visual artist Mel Vera Cruz, whose work incorporates traditional Philippine history images and religious iconography, with elements from popular culture.

ᴗ

I think of myself as a lifelong learner, and I love and appreciate this long process of recovery, though some may tell me it is not mine to recover. I admire that among my community of fellow writers and artists, we learn and engage in recovery work from our families' talkstory traditions and from one another – I love asking what stories their elders told them. I love what we share. And I love bringing this work to my students, many who are Filipino Americans who come into the critical learning spaces that are my classrooms because they are hungry for, in need of connection to Filipino cultures. They want to understand something about themselves and their families. It's really very straight forward. We come to these narratives because we want to learn something about ourselves, that living in this country refuses to teach us. All of this to say, salamat, Christina, for seeing me. Salamat for your kapwa.

Ingat,
bjr

On Being an Immigrant Poet in America

Imagine an entire culture that is passed down for thousands and thousands of years through the spoken word and narrative, so the whole of experience is put into narrative form – this is how the people know who they are as a people, and how individuals learn who they are. — Leslie Marmon Silko

I immigrated to San Francisco in 1973; I was two years old. My parents had previously moved here, in 1969. They rented a small unit in an apartment building near Mitchell's Ice Cream in the Mission District, decades before the area became hip. My mother flew back to Manila in 1971 and gave birth to me. She returned to San Francisco, leaving me and my older sister in the care of our grandparents, aunts, and teenage uncle, who we thought was our older brother. My parents dove into the American grind, saved up, and two years later, my sister and I arrived here, into the arms of our parents, two people we did not know.

The story I've always been told is that back in Manila, and sensing our impending departure, I hid my uncle's car keys under my grandmother's spinster sister's bed, and that upon arriving in a dreary and rainy San Francisco, I cried for days and days. A trip to Disneyland did not assuage me. Other stories of that time entail me throwing up and ruining the interior of my mom's brand-new Toyota Celica.

My parents, hardworking immigrants that they were, bought their first home a couple of years later. We moved to the suburbs, Fremont, to be

exact, just north of Silicon Valley before it became widely known as
Silicon Valley, and where we had a backyard, a cat, and a garden. My
grandmother came from the Philippines, lived with us, and took care
of us as both my parents worked. In the 1970s in Fremont, among my
classmates' parents, my mom was one of the only moms who actually
worked full time. My sisters and I attended private schools, took
Honors English, Advanced Placement History, and Calculus. We
scored high on the SATs, attended big (maybe even prestigious)
universities. Decades later, we are paying mortgages and property taxes.

I tell you this story, not to brag, but to give you an idea of what I
think was my parents' American Dream. And I am thinking about
this American Dream, and American Dream as mythology, because I
am thinking about being an "immigrant poet." Stories about my
family and the English language, of my parents being apprehensive to
speak English in public spaces, of me being tongue tied hence shy
and bookish around my American classmates, all of these stories
belong in the realm of mythology now.

And that's what's happened to my poetry. It's entered the realm
of mythology.

My interest in writing about "the homeland," and "my culture," has
not faded in my four decades of privileged American living, or in my
two decades of writing and publishing in this country, or in my three
years immersed in my MFA program, and not because of nostalgia or
familial obligation.

My history, and my family history have always had documents and
artifacts: posed and candid photographs, home movies, report cards,

detention slips we forged with my parents' signatures, diplomas and degrees, marriage certificates, evidence of immunization, naturalization papers, Philippine and American passports, Facebook posts, and Instagram accounts.

My family history also has its share of lore and folklore. Oral tradition has ruled our self-knowledge, and with oral tradition has come multiple, sometimes quarreling, versions of "truth"; has come hearsay, from which all those wonderful stories that begin, "I wasn't there, but I heard that..."; has come this wonderful phenomenon called tsismis (chisme, gossip), in which everyone gets to speak, some with authority, some with the power of speculation, some only under the condition of anonymity.

This is the largely subjective, undocumented substance that interests me — the quarreling, multiple versions and interpretations of events, reliable and unreliable narrators, secret tellers, disavowers, eyewitnesses, fabricators, yarnspinners. Rather than dismiss any of these artful tellers, I think of how much they must know, what wisdom they contain and how much they withhold, either because nobody has ever asked, or because the message they have accepted and internalized is that their stories are not legitimate, that they are petty and superfluous, because their stories do not conform to the master narrative.

Oral tradition has made me suspicious of single, authoritative texts and master narratives. Instead, I am drawn to what persists and survives despite mainstream cultural insistence upon single, authoritative texts. I love and value the stories in which asides lead to more asides, tangents lead to more tangents, oftentimes with no hope of returning to the original narrative. Consider that sometimes, the narrative asides and tangents are indeed the point of the story.

To be a poet is to be a very good listener. To be a poet is to piece together some kind of musical or artful narrative from official and unofficial documents and undocuments, and to do so in all languages available to me.

Most importantly, I have come to know that some stories take decades before they are ever told, and that in order for me to ever have access to these stories, I must offer something to initiate the exchange. I recently told my now retired mother about one of my dreams, in which her deceased father appeared. I told her this, not in any kind of formal setting, but while she was sweeping the kitchen floor. In return, she told me about how her mother, my grandmother, once had dream foretelling her own miscarriage. This miscarriage was not something I ever knew. Some stories must wait decades to be told, and when they arrive, they do so spontaneously.

None of what I have written here is specific to Filipino immigrant poets in America. But perhaps it can be said that my work ethic and aesthetic preferences as an immigrant in America emphasize exchange/ sharing, hearing and writing multiple voices speaking simultaneously.

To Decenter English

Lately, I have been asking myself, what would it look like, to truly decenter English in my poetry?

As is frequently noted about my poetry, it is multilingual, incorporating Spanish, modern Tagalog, and Baybayin/pre-hispanic Tagalog script into its predominantly English poetic body. "Incorporate," indicates subsumption, assimilation into a dominant body. This is problematic and insufficient to me, as the body is still identified as an English one. Other non-English elements are viewed as ancillary, and even embellishment. I used to think that not italicizing the "foreign" words in my poems was a form of dissent that would challenge the reader's assumptions of foreignness. I continue not to italicize, though these days, I question whether that affects readers' perceptions at all.

And so we must question English. A quick internet search will tell you that Filipinos have been ruled in English since 1898, and instructed in English since 1901. Question though, whether Filipinos are fluent in English — what constitutes fluency, what qualifies as fluency, especially in a (post)(neo)colonially stratified society — or whether Filipinos know enough English in order to mimic, but more so to be ruled and instructed, to execute basic commands. Question also: Which English? Whose English? The poet Jaime Jacinto once used the term, "subtracted bilingual," to describe people like us, our fluency in our elders' tongues disrupted by American education. Look up: Tag-lish. Code Switch. But do not assume all Filipinos are Tagalog speakers.

Question understanding, comprehension, readability – question whose understanding, whose comprehension. Readability for whom?

I was raised and almost exclusively educated in the USA (I spent one semester at University of the Philippines at Diliman), and still, these questions of language do pertain to me. For many of my parents' and other elders' generations of Philippine emigrants, I have learned they never feel entirely "at home" in English. My interactions and communications with them exist in a perpetual state of translation, or in some kind of third space. We collaborate, oftentimes clumsily, in an effort to agree upon meanings. Much of our system of communication is comprised of gesture, tone, and volume. Mostly, we remain in various states of disconnect. Can my poetry ever reach them, and if not, then have I failed as a poet.

In college, I took two semesters of Tagalog language classes. While I would like to think these classes helped bridge some of this aforementioned disconnect, we also learned a formal Tagalog that felt socially strange to employ. *"Ikinagagalak ko pong makilala kayo,"* for example, was not a phrase anyone I knew ever used. Perhaps it amused my parents to hear me say such things, though they themselves would simply say, "Nice to meet you."

In the 1990s, I was introduced to the songs of Quezon City based songwriter Joey Ayala, who hails from the island of Mindanao in the Southern Philippines, a non-Tagalog speaking region. Around this same time, I was also introduced to the Philippine film, *Sakay* (Raymond Red, 1993). What struck me then was that the language of Ayala's songs and Red's cinematic dialogues was a Tagalog so poetic and deep, such words I had never heard before. I wanted to use these in my poetry. They were so beautiful.

But as my parents' generation were educated in English (see above, re: fluency), and had lived in America for decades. I learned I could not assume my parents could even access the meanings of such "deep" words. To quote my father, whom I think of as fluent in Tagalog, definitely more "at home" in Tagalog than in English: "No, we never use those words," and "no, those are not words that I know."

Today, what it means for me to be stuck between languages, and what it means for my father to be stuck between languages are two different things entirely. I want to say I write for my parents. Up until the day he died, my father never read my poetry. I can't take this personally.

So then we must also question: Which Tagalog? Whose Tagalog? And how thick and impenetrable is that colonial residue which has made Filipinos ignorant of their own Mother Tongues? (Though, to be fair, American speakers of various creole Englishes experience alienation from "standard," "formal," "academic," "institutional" English.)

I grew up in a household that spoke and/or listened in Tagalog, Ilocano, and English interchangeably. Code switch is our real lingua franca. Addressee has always been a factor deciding which language and combination of languages to employ — for inclusion, but also exclusion (*Tayo* or *kami? Atin* or *amin?*), tracking who does *not* understand which languages, and who understands how much or how little of each language. This is how you tell "secrets." This is how you *tsismis* (*chisme/gossip*). Perhaps this is why some monolingual folks harbor suspicion for those of us who (must) operate in multiple languages, who appear to flow unimpeded between them. What slippery motives we must have. What wily Filipinos we all are.

To further complicate language, I know very few Filipinos and Filipino Americans who actually read Baybayin, which I had never seen nor heard of until college. My parents had never seen it either. I never knew the Philippines had its own systems of writing (of which the Tagalog Baybayin is just one); this is also colonial mentality, the uncritical assumption that the West brought us literacy and literature. A quick internet search may tell you that pre-conquest, Baybayin was written on impermanent materials (tree bark, bamboo), and used for such things as personal letters and poetry. These days, Baybayin seems to be more of a thing to be looked at. We tattoo the symbols on our bodies, and so then we must translate our bodies upon demand.

A colleague in graduate school once said to me, "Don't use foreign language just because you *can*," and I swear, I wanted to lunge across the table at him and to sink my fist into his smug, white, hipster face for his tone of inconvenience. But it is offensive also to be told that it's as simple as writing in whichever one language I am most comfortable with. *Either* English *or* Tagalog. That too tidy to be realistic "or" is what I resent, am constantly resisting, and ultimately, would like to decenter. And this is why my speakers and personae are constantly composing polyglot lyric, breaking and reconfiguring language, translating and mistranslating, forking their tongues.

What's This Thing About Orientals Together On A Bus

"Well, here we are, Orientals together on a bus."

—Hisaye Yamamoto, *Seventeen Syllables*

"Oriental was a rug that everyone steps on, so we ain't no Orientals.
We were Asian American."

—Richard Aoki

"They did so at the expense of all of us. Un-
controlled capitalism has pushed all of the non-
white people into a social position that only
manual jobs with subhuman pay are open to them.
Consequently, we have been psychologically so
conditioned by the blue-eye-blonde-hair standard
that many of us have lost our perspective.

"We can only survive if we know our place' --
shut up and accept what we are given. We resent
this kind of domination and we are determined to
change it.

Barbara Jane Reyes
4 hrs · 🌐

I remember this young Pinay writer taking a POC writing workshop a while back; the POC instructor told them they shouldn't write about anything "ethnic," not language, not food, not family, not nation, and so forth. And this Pinay writer had nothing to write about that she cared about. And when she told me this, I was like, what kind of stupid bullshit is that. And how does that make you a better writer. And what kind of self-denial and bullshit self-erasure we inculcate our young writers with, as we insist upon fashioning them in tepid **#PoBiz** image. And I wonder how much of this is petty ass insecure as fuck "mentors" trying to squash their future "competition."

Barbara Jane Reyes
3 hrs · 🌐

Sigh. Where I am at, trying to bring attention to Pinay and Pilipinx American poets, most times to no avail, and then where everyone's gawking, at some white dude published at The Nation, writing in bad, really really bad "black vernacular." First, why is this a surprise anymore? Also, Po Biz people, sometimes I really hate you for your exercises in futility, i.e. letting those poets take all your energy, to the detriment of voices that could use amplification.

Barbara Jane Reyes

LOL I love how institutions are trying to take credit for this alleged "rise" in poetry readership. It's not the gatekeepers who make poetry "popular," because, well, they're gatekeepers, i.e. they restrict access. It's the people, who have always had poetry in their lives, in ways that gatekeepers don't recognize as legitimate, worthy poetry.

1.

"Asian American Literature" had already arrived. Just like José Garcia Villa wrote, "Have come, am here." It arrived a long time ago. It was and is chanted by Native Pacific Islanders though "Asian American" does not explicitly include them. It was written on the walls of Angel Island detention centers. It was performed — spoken and sung — at labor movement demonstrations along the West Coast. Nobody rolled out a welcome mat. Everyone was too busy telling it to shut the fuck up; no one gave it permission to speak. They told it to go back to where it came from. By "back to where it came from," they didn't mean Watsonville, Walnut Grove, Yakima, Spokane, SoMa, the Fillmore, Delano, Locke, Temple, Kearny, or El Dorado Streets.

Cf. Hikaru Sulu in *Star Trek IV: The Voyage Home*, as their Klingon war bird descends upon 20th century San Francisco, before the USS Enterprise crew find themselves shell-shocked on Columbus and Kearny Street, down the street from City Lights Books, a block away from the hole in the ground we once knew as the I-Hotel, now the Manilatown Heritage Foundation. Did you catch that? "San Francisco, I was born there." It's a small moment, unimportant to some; did you catch it? (Sulu be droppin #truth in baritone.)

"Asian American Literature" was dissected, its parts duly catalogued in the academy — sojourning and settling, nostalgia (grandmothers, food porn, melancholia, filial piety), emasculated males, and identity crises. I once spoke on a "Hyphenated-American" panel at AWP; when I told those in attendance the first thing I learned in Ronald Takaki's Asian American History class my freshman year at UC Berkeley was to omit that hyphen, because omitting the hyphen indicates we are multiple things, people's eyes were large as the plates on which I used to eat my Lola's pancit. People scribbled in their Moleskines.

I never called either of my grandmothers "Lola." Neither of them was known for making pancit.

Cf. Marlon Fuentes, *Bontoc Eulogy*. American scientists prodding the bodies of Philippine natives, poking their buttocks with sticks, documenting the inward turn of Igorot toes. American voyeurs donning their Sunday best, getting their rocks off watching natives perform fake authenticity, thus enabling other people to pimp their "authenticity."

2.

I have been thinking a lot about, asking myself who I write for. I keep coming back to the 19 year old Pinay student who enters my classroom, and for the first time in her life, sees herself in a work of literature. This image of her many selves is complex, sometimes resilient and dignified, sometimes acting out because she is traumatized, and because she is not content with the limited options afforded to her. Sometimes these Pinay characters and narrators are clear and articulate, sometimes respectful, and sometimes, yes, they are royal bitches who need to be smacked in the mouth.

I have so many students who are these actual 19 year old Pinays, for the first times in their lives, seeing themselves in works of literature. You see how wide their eyes get reading *To Love as Aswang*, where they learn about Sweetie, the internet avatar Filipina girl designed to catch online sexual predators. They cry when in *Invocation to Daughters*, they learn about a teenage Pinay from Washington, who commit suicide after her father shamed her on YouTube. They learn about a young Pinay in Monterey County, whose husband cut her into pieces and dumped her parts in garbage bags. Some of my students step back as they approach shut down; this is too close, too real. This tells too much truth. This tells the "outside world" about our baggage. This shows us what the "outside world" thinks of us.

Rather than shut down though, they start asking questions. How come Filipinas are viewed and treated this way. How come I haven't heard about these girls and women. How come they weren't on the news. Who else do we not know about. This is what they want from "our" works of literature. This is why I write. This is for whom I write.

And so I push. I say, we can and need to do more, we need to check ourselves, not just teach the works of our literary coterie to MFA students. We need to get more of our work about us into the world, into the hands of more and more young and hungry readers farther outside of institutions, outside of our comfort zones. Let's challenge expectation, I say, fuck institutions that would rein us in. They are not my priority. A fellow Asian American author then cut me off and tried to shut me down, mansplaining that just trying to teach the works of our friends is enough, that my way of doing things was "reckless, destructive, and dangerous." And I was like, what the hell does that mean. And then I was like, unfollow, unfriend.

3.

I'm the last "Asian American" author you'd want to ask about "Asian American" Literature. "Asian American" editors of "Asian American" publications, even the ones who specifically solicit my work, don't publish me as much as Latinx editors do. My writing is never quite what "Asian American" editors are looking for. It's ugly. It's edgy. It could be that pesky Spanish colonialism that gave me my tendency towards art and rebellion performed *con todo forma*, and my unapologetic code switching. I was raised Catholic by generations of demonstrative Third World Catholics. All than Lenten darkness, all my clashing and warring against patriarchs and machismo (see above, re: "mansplained"), have unfiltered my filters, and have informed my aesthetics, tone, and volume. All those curses and prayers, countless novenas recited by the rosary clutching matrons of my clans, have insisted upon processions, wailing spectacles in my poems, these fucking Via Dolorosas and Agnus Deis.

Those are my poetic lines.

My mentors incited me. Liturgies, Stations of the Cross, the rosary are forms! Go to Tagalog mass at Saint Patrick Church, Good Friday Spanish mass at Mission Dolores, la Virgen de Guadalupe procession! Read Murguía, Arteaga, Galeano! Juan Felipe Herrera, Jimmy Santiago Baca! Read Anzaldúa again, always! More Lorca! And so I wrote *Poeta en San Francisco*.

My husband, poet Oscar Bermeo introduced me to the poetries of Julia de Burgos, Jack Agüeros, Miguel Piñero, Pedro Pietri, and Urayoán Noel. He gifted me with poetry by Victor Hernández Cruz and Adrian Castro. This was the poetry I did not know I needed.

I'm the last "Asian American" author you'd want to ask about "Asian American" Literature. Though I have been teaching and curriculum developing multiple iterations of Filipinx and APIA Literature courses in San Francisco based universities for over a decade now, I am not a scholar, and I do not write scholarly essays. I am a literary practitioner, I am an adjunct professor, and I am a hustler. You will see me rushing on public transit from my full time public health desk job to my enormous evening classes on the other side of the bay, crafting lecture notes, lesson planning, and grading between work projects and writing projects. I don't have the luxury of time and mental space to theorize this field.

4.

We are celebrating the 50th birthday of "Asian American."

According to his 2002 obituary in the *Los Angeles Times*, Yuji Ichioka of the Asian American Political Alliance, a student org created in 1968, coined the term "Asian American."

"Asian American" has its roots in activism and revolutionary movements. Since then, other terms have come into popular use — APA, APIA, Asian Diaspora — to reflect the growth, global movement, and changing politics of a community that is really many different communities, bursting at the seams with so many different, if not conflicting ideologies and aesthetics.

"Asian American" could still be relevant, or useful, but wouldn't it be nice — and smart — if folks who speak this term like the gospel actually knew where the term came from, and why it was necessary to speak this term into existence. I am in Oakland, combing through the [online] FBI Vault for information. I'm proud to see my former professors' names here. I'm proud to see my elders as young activists, fearlessly speaking of "Yellow Power," and "Revolution," in a time of FBI surveillance and infiltration. Even their art was surveilled.

"Asian Americans" allied themselves with the Black Panther Party and other revolutionary orgs of the 1960s — according to his obituary, Ichioka did not agree with Huey Newton's politics, but publicly demonstrated in support of Newton at his trial nonetheless. "Asian

Americans" were vocally anti-war, anti-colonialist, and anti-imperialist; they were disruptors, and I am proud to have been educated by those who came from these movements.

We expect the term "Asian American" to do so much, without having much common understanding amongst ourselves. I realize my own impatience with "Asian American" is complicated. There are its obvious ethnic limitations, i.e. reflecting the ethnic demographics of its 1968 activist population. There are its obvious limitations with national origin, complexities and diversity of each ethnicity, and political history — Chinese American is not "from China," is not Taiwanese is not Southeast Asian is not Tagalog speaker is not Pacific Islander. There's just too fucking much to stuff into "Asian American."

In other words, fifty years later, "Asian American," is enormous and meaningless, which is why we push for disaggregation of our data. Why do we still expect the term "Asian American Literature" to do everything for us.

5.

Remember when the Poetry Foundation's "Asian American" poets list caused a national, emotional internet fracas. Resounding cries of "why wasn't I included," broke my social media feeds. And thus was spawned a private Facebook group of "Asian American" writers, and a Google Doc for all to add their own names and their friends' names, to submit to the Poetry Foundation. This ordeal made me more cynical. Why are we reliant upon institutions such as the Poetry Foundation to give us our worth and determine our meaning. Why do we give these others the power define us. Do we think this is the only way that we will become visible to our own communities. And isn't this a problem as well.

Because "Asian American" has been appropriated and defanged, I am suspicious of and adversarial to contemporary "Asian American" canon-making. By whom and for whom is a canon of "Asian American" literature created? What is considered "acceptable" for this canon? Whose standards and criteria are these? Whose complexities do we decide to ignore or erase? For whose gaze must you write, and in whose language, by whose politics must you abide, what credentials must you acquire, in order to be considered for inclusion. We must question what kind of work, whose work, is omitted, and why. If we built our bodies of work from the ground-up, if we built up our work in the communities we grew up in, rather than in our MFA programs and summer writing retreats, if we were to re-envision something other than canon-making institutions' inclusion, what would it be.

6.

"A political poem need not be oversimplified, rhetorical or temporary."
　　　　—Serafin Syquia, "Politics and Poetry," *Liwanag* (1975).

Al Robles wrote, "The best part of our poetry is our struggle, and the best part of our struggle is our poetry." Do read his meditative essay "Hanging on to the Carabao's Tail," in *Amerasia Journal* (1989). Manong Al was among the best of us, because his poems came from the voices of the historically exploited and erased, to whom he listened so finely, and with so much respect. But you won't hear Manong Al's name mentioned in many national discussions of "Asian American Literature." It's scrappy. It's "street." It isn't trying to be respectable. And yet, it is artful, infused with the rhythms of labor camps and field work, of taxi dance halls, of beatdowns and race riots, of aging, dreaming, and dying.

The world in which we live, work, and write is messy, and it is full of injustice and violence; it needs us to bring our ruckus. We are at our best when we are scrappy; when we are noisy and unruly, unashamed of profanity, irreverence, and taboo.

Some of the most interesting works of "Asian American Literature" thrive in the world of indie publishing and micro presses, where you will find our authors experimenting, prolific, testifying, refusing to conform to any single "Asian American" canonical representation or well-behaved institutional standards. They have flipped their well-appointed writing desks and throw chairs. They write protest poems, performance texts, redactions and erasures, disaster capitalism poetics, polyglot, hip-hop, graphic narrative, comix, spec fic, YA lit, 21st century remythologizing, they genre and gender cross, bastardize, lyricize, holler, diatribe, pray, protest, decenter, transgress, decolonize, wail in lament, invent language, code switch like a motherfucker. As Tina Bartolome has written, they "mess with hegemony."

7.

I have taught MFA workshop and seminar at Mills College and University of San Francisco. My MFA students are diverse in culture, ethnicity, economics, migration, and gender identity. They dislike navel gazing and coyness. They dislike cleverness for sake of itself. They appreciate experimentation when it is useful, when it reveals something big, something urgent, something is at stake. They loved Truong Tran, his use of the prose poetry form, his expansion (explosion?) of the line, his poetry's queerness. They loved Rajiv Mohabir's polyglot, folk, talkstory "chutney" poems of *The Cowherd's Son.*

More regularly, I teach Pinay and Filipino Literature classes at University of San Francisco, and Filipino and Asian American Literature classes at San Francisco State University, where I find huge classrooms full of students from almost everywhere in Asia and everywhere in the world, who couldn't care less who got their MFA where, and who studied under which sizzling hot NYC poets. They don't care about AWP, the Poetry Foundation, the Academy of American Poets, and other canon-making American institutions into which we clamber and clamor to gain entrance. They care about seeing themselves in literature, and they care about resonance.

My students are the children of refugees. They are English language learners. They grew up translating for their elders, in shopping centers, in banks, in doctors' offices. They are nursing students and bank tellers. My students are workers and working parents. They are hustling multiple gigs to pay for college.

We read *Tomorrow's Memories*, the diary of Angeles Monrayo, and the Op Eds of Helen Rillera, which Jean Vengua has recovered and reprinted. These are "non-literary" (or "extra-literary"?) Pinays writing themselves out of the previous century's historical invisibility, though they shouldered all the community's and family's reproductive labor. We discuss the epistolary, where and when women and girls even have the time, space, and permission to write.

We read *Corpse Watching*, the TinFish Press chapbook of the incarcerated poet Sarith Peou, and Monica Sok's essay, "Fear, Fearlessness, and Intergenerational Trauma." We discuss what and how the next generation inherit what they do, as we also talk about what the survivors in their own families do not talk about. And as we make the clear distinctions between immigrant and refugee statuses, they get how dishonest it is for news media to insist upon labelling the current waves of refugees "migrants."

We read Gene Luen Yang's graphic novel *American Born Chinese*, and have to confront Cousin Chin-Kee. Is this how Americans see us? Is this what we think of our ethnic selves? Why have we insisted on internalizing this archaic image of the "Heathen Chinee." How do we make peace with Cousin Chin-Kee?

When students tell me they have never read a book authored by someone of Filipino or Asian descent, I think, by college, especially with upperclassmen, it's already almost too late. Many sit silently wide-eyed in my classrooms, and then at the end of the semester, hug me, thank me profusely, and do not want to leave. This tells me the work has resonated.

In addition to working full time, in addition to adjunct professor gigs, in addition to writing my own books, I have carved out time to work with the San Francisco based non-profit Philippine American Writers and Artists (PAWA), in curating free local events for writers, at community venues such as Eastwind Books of Berkeley, owned by Harvey and Bea Dong; the blackbox Bindlestiff Studio, "the Epicenter of Filipino American Performing Arts"; and the South of Market Bayanihan Center, which also houses the Pinay-owned independent bookstore, Arkipelago Books. We co-produce events with the librarian of the San Francisco Public Library's Filipino American Center, and with the Yuchengco Philippine Studies Program at University of San Francisco. We also hold events at the Philippine Consulate, where the Consul General opens each event with a formal welcome speech.

We do this work as volunteers, and oftentimes, with no budget but some private donations that come in every now and then. We do this because there has not been a consistent space for Filipino writers since Bay Area Pilipino American Writers (BAPAW) — Shirley Ancheta, Jeff Tagami, Jaime Jacinto, among others — ceased to exist, despite our large numbers in the San Francisco Bay Area. We have made ourselves look tremendous, using social media. We're really a small group of folks who work full time, mostly as educators, who meet regularly and plan shit, usually sitting around a table of lumpia and plates of pancit.

What Does It Mean to be an APIA Author in "These Times"

Let's be clear on this: Xenophobia and racism are not on the rise just now in 2017, in the United States of America. Xenophobia and racism have been here, as our ongoing condition, and many of us APIAs have benefited from them—including from anti-blackness and native genocide.

What I would like to think is changing is our consciousness and the willingness of some in our literary communities to address institutional violence directly in our literary work, in our use of language, and also in our literary career ambitions.

When I am most optimistic, I believe I see an eroding of reticence on the part of some in our literary communities to interrogate our relationship to the State, to the Corporation, to US American institutions, and to power structures that perpetrate violence and terror that are based in gender, sexuality, class, race, religion, ableism, ecology, and immigration.

Questions I have:

- How may we foster in ourselves and one another a willingness to soul search, to ask ourselves why we have been so in denial, going about our lives and writing careers as if we have nothing to do with any of this violence and terror?

- How can we critically examine why we have consented to the role of the well-behaved, respectable Good Colonial, resigned and relegated to apery, when we truly know this will not keep us and our loved ones safe?

- How may we hold ourselves accountable and do the hard work of calling out those in our communities who inflict these violences upon our own?

I would love to see more poetry and literature, more community-based grassroots publishing and mentoring arise from that critical self-examination, and more prioritizing and centering resistance, dissent, and defiance. I have been returning to Carlos Bulosan frequently—to remind me to be present, engaged, vigilant in the world, to remind me not to take "American freedom" for granted.

> "I read more books, and became convinced that it was the duty of the artist to trace the origins of the disease that was festering American life." ~ Carlos Bulosan.

> "...the writer is also a citizen; and as a citizen he must safeguard his civil rights and liberties. Life is a collective work and also a social reality. Therefore the writer must participate with his fellow man in the struggle to protect, to brighten, to fulfill life. Otherwise he has no meaning—a nothing." ~ Carlos Bulosan.

You may want to argue with me that poetry is personal, not political—
that poetry is about beauty and beautiful things. And I would respond
that resistance, dissent, and defiance are beautiful because when we
stand up for what we believe is right, we expose our rawest, truest
selves, and who and what we love most in the world are all laid bare.
Because especially during the most volatile times, compassion, hope,
and light are beautiful.

I would also add that under the rule of tyranny, there is no luxury of
neutrality, of just being.

> "...always art is in the hands of the dominant class – which
> wields its power to perpetuate its supremacy and existence."
> ~ Carlos Bulosan.

> "...in which to be is to be like, and to be like is to be like the
> oppressor..." ~ Paolo Freire.

So then, what does it mean to be an APIA author in these times? To
learn well the necessary activist history of our forebears, to understand
why activism and art have no tidy dividing line between them. To
meaningfully resist white supremacy and patriarchy, to meaningfully
resist the historical pressure and desire to conform to bourgeois ideas,
which do not reflect our own lived realities, and therefore do not
benefit our communities. More insidiously, they mean to undermine
and erase our efforts at self-determination.

We must meaningfully resist appropriation by institutions that would skew and defang our words and work, via tokenism and celebrations of diversity, for example, for their own edification.

The work is daunting, and it is neverending. The smallest start is to read. Here are recommendations: Tarfia Faizullah, Solmaz Sharif, Tony Robles, Janice Sapigao, Sarith Peou. Brandy Nālani McDougall, Rajiv Mohabir, Cheena Marie Lo, Bhanu Kapil, Craig Santos Perez, Aimee Suzara. They're all poets.

"a million brown pilipino faces

chanting: makibaka, makibaka, makibaka

makibaka, makibaka, makibaka..." ~ Al Robles.

"This is poetry as illumination, for it is through poetry that we give name to those ideas which are, until the poem, nameless and formless-about to be birthed, but already felt." ~ Audre Lorde.

I often think of, as a poet, this binary social attitude that poetry is on the one hand frivolous and excessive, and on the other that poetry is so necessary, especially in times of strife and turmoil, such as now. As poets, we are tasked with taking the temperature of the room and putting it down on the page with eloquence. And then as poets, we are accused of being too little in the world, too much in our own indulgent heads, not doing anything of social relevance because we are seen as sitting in our safe little writing studios, agonizing over muses and love.

In the academic world, we aren't seen much at all because we're not perceived as doing any heavy lifting like those who toil over producing factual, institutionally sanctioned bodies of work.

If we are regarded, it is with disdain for being so "poetic," elliptical, and flippant—somehow unserious because of the relative brevity of the poem, because of tone, and because of the genre's artfulness. And because of the oft-made error that even many academics make, that the "I" is not lyric and expansive, but personal and individual, hence small. And that the love poem is always a poem of personal, self-serving eros, certainly not of larger social significance, even when we are guided by the Filipino core value of kapwa, "shared humanity."

> "We must strive every day so that this love of living humanity will be transformed into actual deeds, into acts that serve as examples, as a moving force." ~ Che Guevara.

Wanna Peek Into My Notebook?

Dear Poetas,

Lawrence Ferlinghetti passed away today. Diane di Prima passed away four months ago. Thinking about these two monument poets, I revisit my love for the sprawling song of poem, the poem that sings to us in our natural languages, the poem that is meant to sing aloud. I revisit my ongoing love for City Lights Books and the poetries which have informed the roots of my own public poetics. Mostly, I revisit my participation in public poet life.

These days, "public poet life" means posting on social media. Indeed, you will see me on social media, posting things like this:

On Facebook:

Barbara Jane Reyes
July 31, 2018 · 🌐

•••

All kinds of people will always hate your work, your tone, your manners, your language, your sensibility; people will hate you and wish you would just shut up and disappear. They will wish silence and failure and self-denial upon you. You will always be the wrong everything, the wrong ethnicity, the wrong gender, the wrong age, the wrong schools, the wrong aesthetics, the wrong unfuckwithable status. And you will write anyway, because there will always be the people who have been looking for your work, who have been looking for someone like you to say the things they have always feared saying, to use the languages they have been punished for using, whose lives you've saved or transformed with your work, who are writing books, creating art and performance pieces, because your work has touched, has moved them.

On Twitter:

Barbara Jane Reyes
@bjanepr ···

Reminder: WOC, less reticence and coyness, and more stating clearly and directly what we need, why we need it, and from whom. This is an important exercise in our own deepening understanding of what we need and where we're at, and learning how to be brave enough to articulate it.

8:23 AM · Feb 19, 2021 · Twitter for Android

Barbara Jane Reyes
@bjanepr ···

Reminder: Poetas, this is not a competition. Unlearn this capitalist, scarcity mindset. I am not competing with any of you. I want us all to define and find our own successes, be confident, and thrive. We are all here to build something together. We can have this if we want it.

6:40 AM · Feb 17, 2021 · Twitter for Android

On Instagram:

Barbara Jane Reyes
@bjanepr

Read more poetry. You'll find that poets are doing the kinds of things scholars and academics don't know how to do yet, or aren't brave enough to do yet.

Barbara Jane Reyes
@bjanepr

I was 31 when my first book was published, 33 when I finished my MFA, 34 when I won my one and only "big" literary award, 44 when my dream publisher offered me a book contract. Writing and publishing are lifelong work, with no shortcuts, no single correct path. Be wary of those who say otherwise.

Different platforms, generally similar messages. These posts and memes get "liked" dozens to hundreds of times, re-tweeted, screenshotted, shared. Social media followers and "friends," respond, " ," " ," and "Fuck yeah, girl!" — people reacting to people saying provocative stuff, until a few minutes later, new provocative stuff is said, and the old provocative stuff gets pushed down the page to dissipate in the noise. And then everyone migrates over to the next social media platform.

Around 2001, a friend recommended I start a "web log," which I did on Blogger, to log my writing process and works in progress. Self-conscious of its presence on the world wide web, I didn't log much of anything there at all. I also created my first writer website on Geocities. I returned to my Blogger "web log" in 2003, when my professor Jeffery Paul Chan instructed us to keep a writing journal to respond to his weekly writing prompts. Something about risk and vulnerability occurred to me and I had to learn to overcome this, as anyone online could have found and read my works in progress. After

Professor Chan's class, I continued using that Blogger space, then WordPress (which was more aesthetically pleasing to me) to write about writing, reading, and revising, to collect and compile found materials and ideas for my MFA thesis, *Poeta en San Francisco*. After grad school, I continued with this practice for every book and chapbook I've written, and for every new semester of curriculum development and teaching. I loved this space as incubation space.

I value this public writing as a kind of collaborative writing. It oftentimes garners more interest and interaction than my published poems — poems are beheld as artifacts, whereas social media incubation space is fluid, malleable, always new, giving space for immediate response, where folks can ask questions and have a conversation. When I post drafts of poems I don't know what to do with or where they are going, others feel invited to help me flesh out the work. As I continue meditating on the theme of Pinay poetics, these meditations mean something to the Pinay and Pinxy writers, educators, and students following along. As I think out loud about Filipino Americans and Filipinos in or out of literary spaces, my community is there, thinking out loud with me, sharing their ideas, complicating and challenging mine. We make collaborative pieces, and these can become full blown essays, honest and lyrical. Educators used to send their students to my blog. Now they send their students to my social media. Editors solicit work from me, based upon what they see me posting online. This is how I learned of "platform," that thing you are supposed to build, if you are to become a "successful" author.

Today, "blog" is an antiquated term and practice to those native to current rapid fire social media practice, in which there is just not enough time or space for nuanced thinking. And though I am a poet who values the succinct, being succinct comes from the decades-long practice of a long and slow dailiness, and public space gives me accountability. It is exercise — conditioning, toning the muscles that enable me to be prolific. I begin at the blog with language, phrases, images, lists, questions, bullet points, notes, writing to and through exhaustion, writing past exhaustion, writing until the work is good and done. And then I begin all over again, with the encouragement, input, questions of the trusted folks with whom I have built rapport.

There's an unsavory aspect to all of this as well — trolls, bullies, and generally unreasonable requests for my time in the personal public space. These days, I encounter more people who don't take the time to exchange and dialogue; they want me to notice them, they want me to give them the magic bullets and magic beans in publishing, they make demands in wholly unprofessional ways, all of this uncompensated and immediate. I constantly have to reinforce my boundaries. I miss the fruitful dialogues, the germinating of ideas and cross pollination, the meandering storylines that can occur in our personal public spaces. These days, to avoid the noise, I recede into my non-virtual notebooks, where I continue to tone the writing muscles, longhand with 0.7 mm mechanical pencil on paper. Of the personal public space I've kept, I offer here a peek into my 2010-2020 "notebooks."

ư

I want to begin with a memory of my mother, Evelyn Pulmano Reyes. She passed away on November 23, 2020, and my grief is beyond deep. It's incomprehensible and bottomless. About a month before she passed, she asked me why I'd only given her two of my books, and I couldn't tell her how afraid I was to share my books with her, though she and my father attended many of my early literary events. Today, as I revisit that day a decade ago when I gave her a copy of my third book, *Diwata*, which I dedicated to her father and sister, I am overcome. But I am also consoled that I was able to share my work with her.

August 3, 2010 Diwata: Telling and Writing Family Story

Diwata's toughest reader for me is going to be my mother. Critics, book reviewers, academics, Po-Biz haters got nothing on the fear I felt when I handed my mother her copy of *Diwata*.

She is a reader. She will read my book. Indeed, the people in my family are readers. My mother's friends are also readers; some of them apparently follow my work, and so they will also read *Diwata*. That's pretty awesome, especially when we're always told Filipinos are non-readers and non-book buyers. For me, what is at stake is this: I need my mother to know that my work as a poet is an earnest attempt at paying respect to our elders and ancestors. More concretely, I have dedicated my book to my mother's eldest sister and her father, both of whom are recently deceased, and this gesture really touched her. I want my mother not to be disappointed by what I have written in their memory.

When I was in my early 20's, I attended UP Diliman for one semester, and I spent more time with my Philippines-based extended family than I'd ever before. Then I'd hop on Quezon City jeepneys by myself, speaking my rudimentary American Tagalog, and I would see my dad's city. I'd see the streets' sharp and mischievous young men, cads and players, and I'd think of my dad in their place decades earlier. My cousin, who was a college student at University of San Tomas, my dad's alma mater, and I would joyride at 4 am through Manila, and end up saying hello to the Rizal monument in Luneta Park. I was so dumb and American that I'd call out the security guards trying to bribe us for merienda money when they'd tell us smoking at the monument was a violation subject to exorbitant fines. Still, I wanted to understand my parents' home. My dad still calls the Philippines "home."

For the first time since I was a small child, I spent time at the house where my mother and her siblings grew up; this is the house in Gattaran, Cagayan, just north of Tuguegarao. My mother's father, whom I call Papa, showed me so many old photos, introduced me to so many relatives I didn't remember, verbally placed them in our extensive family tree, and then he told me that it was my responsibility to remember. Papa was really keen that way; he recognized that I was the writer in the family, and that meant something. He was so pleased that I'd come back "home," that I could experience both the city and the provinces firsthand.

As my mother flipped through the pages of *Diwata,* she came across the poem, "A Little Bit About Lola Ilang." "Oh! It's Lola Ilang!" she exclaimed. Lola Ilang was my mother's spinster aunt on my mother's mother's side. Her name was Manuela Adviento. My memories of her are vague but animated, if such a combination is possible. My interactions with her were probably hilarious, given that she didn't speak a word of English, and I'd run at the mouth all the time as a kid. Indeed, it is true, as stated in the poem, that when Lola Ilang died, no one knew how old she was, and that towards the end of her life, she herself had forgotten. I had to wonder, God! What else has Lola Ilang forgotten? How can I try to fill in those memories (should I)? My mother's eldest sister, Tita Alice, and my mother herself, find voice in this poem; they told me stories of Lola Ilang smoking her cigarettes backwards, lit end in mouth, that my mother tried to do this as well, and burnt her tongue. I filled in all kinds of stuff, remembering what I've been told by other older Filipino ladies, about how that tradition may have come about. How does one smoke outside at night and not be seen? How important is this in wartime?

My way into history, folklore, mythology, has been through my elders' stories and their encouragement. As my parents have gotten older, they've started telling me so many stories, stuff I thought they didn't bother with anymore. I'd assumed their decades of working the American Dream, buying a home in the suburbs, sending me and my three sisters to college, had supplanted who we are and where we came from as priorities in their lives.

My lesson here was this: don't assume. Or, don't assume the pragmatic American Dream stuff has made our stories of us less important or less relevant, or has caused them to forget. I got to a certain point in my relationship with my parents that I actually started asking them questions, and I persisted in asking them questions. Imagine that, huh? Actually being able to talk to my Filipino parents, and have them talk to me as a grown-up. I'd tell them what I vaguely remembered from when I was really young in the Philippines. I was so young, and these memories are so dreamy; the Philippines of my childhood memory and imagination is lush and fabulous, magical. Houses are alive and exercise agency. Goats also have intention. The air in the city was so humid and sparkly, swirling thick with ghosts I could almost smell.

This did and did not jibe with the country I saw as a UP Diliman exchange student, taking comparative literature and Philippine anthropology, and with the country I see today. The Cagayan River behind Papa's house has changed its course, and now so many relatives blurred together in my head. I'd look at old photographs of people and ask my parents, this man with the cigar, did he live in a nipa hut behind Papa's house on the way to the river? Who was he? How come the house isn't there anymore? Where did he go? Why is the river so close to the back of the house? It didn't used to be like this; am I remembering this right? Indeed, many of the elders in my family are loving these questions, and volunteering all kinds of narratives. The boys in the provinces were not as forthcoming, and I had to be more persistent.

Certainly, having a book entitled *Diwata* has led my parents to ask me how much I do know or remember about Philippine mythologies, and how much I understand; this makes me a little fearful as well. What if I've got it all wrong? What if they don't appreciate all of my own narrative filling in, my geographic, cultural, and poetic departures from the original stories? Still, they've been helpful, especially with translation and explanation of names and terms. I don't think they see it as my getting it right or wrong. I think they also appreciate that I recognize their stories and their memories as important, and defining, worthy of being documented, worthy of becoming art.

April 28, 2011 Towards a Pinay "We" Poetics

I am interested in "we" poetics. "We" is a persona in which I've been writing for a long time now, and even my "I" is a "we." This came to my attention fully when poet Nathaniel Mackey articulated this "we," in his discussion about the ongoing emergence journey of a people in his serial poem, "Song of the Andoumboulou." This "we" appeals to me as a Filipina; I was raised in a culture of "we." The Tagalog terms pakikisama and bayanihan speak to me about the social value of this 'we' in practice. We are valued as members of a larger whole, in interaction and relation to others within this larger whole. We know ourselves as members of a larger whole, in interaction and relation to others within this larger whole.

Poetically, I also come from a tradition of a "we"; think of the community organizer, activist Filipino American poets Carlos Bulosan and Al Robles. While Robles wrote in *Rappin' With Ten Thousand Carabaos in the Dark*, about and in the voices of the Manongs, the West Coast Filipino American migrant laborers of the early twentieth century, a socialism-oriented Bulosan invoked Whitmanesque multitudes of working men in "If You Want to Know What We Are." I, too, have attempted to write as "the people," this Filipino multitude:

We, Malakas and Maganda

We, Moluccas and Magellan

We, Devil and Dogeater

We, Starfruit and Sampaguita

We, Malakas and Maganda

We, Pepe and Pilar

We, Devil and Dogeater

We, Coconut and Crab

We, Malakas and Maganda

We, Eskinol and ESL

We, Devil and Dogeater

We, Igorot and Imelda

We, Malakas and Maganda

We, B-boy and Bulosan

We, Devil and Dogeater

We, Subic Bay and Stockton

We, Malakas and Maganda

We, Gangsta Rap and Galleon Trade

We, Devil and Dogeater

We, Comfort Woman and Carabao

We, Malakas and Maganda

We, Lea Salonga and Lapu-Lapu

We, Devil and Dogeater

We, TnT and Taguba

We, Malakas and Maganda

I think of this poem as conventionally "masculine"; I am acutely
aware that I have already cited more male poets speaking as "the
people," as I try to write about Pinay "we" poetics. I have previously
written an essay on women of color and reticence. I reject reticence as
a natural state, and instead witness women writers of color ignored,
or bullied into the interior provinces of the domestic, the personal,
and private, while the men charge themselves with handling the
"official story," representing "the people," addressing the outside
world. Ultimately, many women are barred from being so ambitious
as to speak on that "too big" outside world, effectively silenced. This
is one contradiction I am trying to unravel; the fine details of our
everyday lives comprise a human being, communities of human
beings, and the cultures of communities of human beings in the
world. Writing these details then, should be regarded as ambitious.

With my third book, *Diwata*, I was centrally concerned with myth-
making. I thought about how to write a Pinay version of Leslie
Marmon Silko's *Storyteller*, which was, along with a stack of books by
Eduardo Galeano, a springboard for *Diwata*, as I tried to write in the
voices of elder storytellers, to remember the stories they told, and the
ones they never told me. What intimate, unwritten knowledge, what
"unofficial story," do we hold in our memories and private spaces?
What stories do we know in our bones, from having heard them so

many times? What stories do we all collaboratively participate in telling? As women, how do these old mythic stories of mermaids and aswangs still hold relevance in the 21st century? Do we still need them (the stories, the tellers, the mermaids, and aswangs)? What responsibility do we have to be the bearers and tellers of story, especially since many of these elder storytellers have passed away?

Now, we are in danger of becoming disconnected, brown-skinned, immigrant American girls and women, living in American cities, besieged by a technology that may or may not facilitate our coming together as community and family in our sacred gathering spaces, our kitchen tables, our campfires and hearths. Revisiting Joy Harjo's poem, "Perhaps the World Ends Here," reminds us why these spaces are so important:

> This table has been a house in the rain, an umbrella in the sun.

> Wars have begun and ended at this table. It is a place to hide in the shadow of terror. A place to celebrate the terrible victory.

> We have given birth on this table, and have prepared our parents for burial here.

I have so many questions. If we are a "we," then can the single-author book become one of our tables and hearths, sacred gathering spaces in which we may all collaboratively participate in storytelling.

As Pinays, we constantly resist silence; many of us know the pain of having been mothered by silenced women. From within a culture of we, silence can be construed as consent, and dissent as an inconvenience, an undesirable alien element undermining consensus and community. To dissent and to demand is to be a bitch. We dissent, we are privately thanked and publicly alienated, as other women police the public boundaries of acceptable thought, social behavior, and speech. It breaks my heart, because we know experientially that we cannot afford not to speak our piece in a world that so casually labels us Pinays as nannies, maids, "bar girls," mail order brides, various girls who service you. This is obscene and offensive, identifying all Filipino women as consenting, purchasable bodies in this commerce.

My second book, *Poeta en San Francisco*, rails against the international commerce of Filipina bodies, that expectation of being serviced, as has emerged from military, Christian, cultural, economic invasions of the islands. This commerce relies upon the denigration of the Pinay from her original position of social, religious, and civic power, and it relies upon her silence construed as consent. *Poeta en San Francisco* rejects that silence (negates that construed consent) by aggressively indicting the Christian missionary, the American soldier, the sex tourist, the Asiaphile, those benefiting from our dehumanization; my position here is often called, "white man hating":

[why choose pilipinas, remix]

the answer is simple, my friend. pilipinas are noteworthy for their beauty, grace, charm. they are especially noted for their loyalty. their nature is sun sweetened. their smiles downcast, coy. pilipinas possess intrinsic beauty men find delightful and irresistible. pilipinas are family-oriented by essence, resourceful, devoted. what's more, english is the true official language of the pilipinas, so communication is uncomplicated. and even though some believe in the old ways, the majority of the pilipinas are christian, so you are assured they believe in the one true god you do. foreign, but not too foreign, they assimilate quickly and they do not make a fuss. in short, the pilipinas are custom tailored to fit your diverse needs.

now will that be cash or charge?

I culled the above text, "found poetry" from a Filipina mail order bride website; it is actual testimonial from satisfied customers, serving as marketing material for those men on the fence about purchasing a Filipina over girls from other impoverished nations.

I am a poet because I believe poems can effectively resist silence, and I believe in, as June Jordan has written, poetry as a humanizing project. In writing against the Filipina mail order bride dehumanization demonstrated above, the self-representation should be truly collective, not spoken in an imposed, singular Pinay voice silencing other Pinay voices.

If we collaboratively participate in the telling, then what does that look and sound like? That's what I wanted to try to write next. I began to wonder whether overcoming Pinay silence could be as simple as asking a group of Pinays a series of questions, and opening up the space to answer. I have followed Bhanu Kapil's example of gathering questionnaire responses from other South Asian women for her book, *The Vertical Interrogation of Strangers.* In her introduction, Kapil writes, "Is it possible for you to say the thing you have never been able to say, even to the one you have spent your whole life loving?" She aimed for an uncensored "honest and swift" text, and I'd wondered if any conditions we set up could really ensure such pure, unmediated results.

I was also influenced by Claire Kageyama-Ramakrishnan's poem, "One Question, Several Answers," in which an unseen speaker asks the same one question, "Where did your father live?" again and again. The addressee appears to have no choice but to keep answering. From her responses to this persistent questioning, a picture of her father's life in the WWII Japanese internment camps emerges, gains color, dimension, detail, and sadness.

I posted a call for participants on various Filipino artist and community listservs, and many Pinays wrote back to me, not to participate or to voice any opinion on the project. They wrote to me to make their presence known, either as private gestures of solidarity, or so that I could acknowledge them, which confirmed for me the need to be visible (or to overcome invisibility), and to be heard (or to overcome silence or being silenced).

I was disappointed but not surprised at the small number of Pinays who voiced interest in participating, and in the smaller number of Pinays who followed through, and responded to my questions about body, self-image, mothering, daughtering, home, voice, worry, and ritual. What I wanted to know: If we can speak for ourselves, then what are we saying about ourselves, how do we represent ourselves, what is privately and socially important to us. What's really eating at us when we're looking in the mirror, preoccupied with applying lipstick, dreading going on a diet, before we rush off to the next errand, task, or chore.

In the spirit of Anne Waldman's "Fast Speaking Woman," and her predecessor María Sabina, I have come to craft these Pinay responses into trance-like, incantatory bursts. In the spirit of *Diwata*, woman's voice is wind, woman's body is earth; woman is muse, deity, and poet, and these responses become woman-centric genealogies, prayers to our mothers and to ourselves:

> Daughter of reinvented selves, she of the new names.
>
> Daughter of Evangeline la Reina, daughter of Eve.
>
> Daughter of Maria la China, she of the rice powdered face.
>
> Daughter of Praxedes Adviento, she with the tree trunk arms.
>
> Daughter of Trinidad y Adoracion, storytellers who do not speak.
>
> Daughter of Everilda, lady of sharp tongued gossip.
>
> Daughter of Rufina, maker of dresses, lover of orchids.
>
> Daughter of Florentina, pursued by American soldiers.
>
> Daughter of Leyteño peasant, daughter of .22 long rifle.
>
> [...]
>
> Daughter of Morena, we lift our eyes to the sun.
>
> Daughter of Kayumanggi, we warm ourselves in your earth.

Litany, participatory prayer and procession, has been one of my organizing principles; repetition as affirmation, reinforcement, assertion, and public demonstration.

Mother of mother's compassion.

Mother of are you eating enough.

Mother of put that away.

Mother of clean this up.

Mother of make your bed.

Mother of do your homework.

Mother of shut off the lights.

Mother of you're so beautiful.

I am interested in these prayer-like forms elevating the domestic work which has been used to debase and silence us, as in Irene Faye Duller's words, "I am the maid of the world, and the world has made me dirty." Can we also be multitudes of Pinays, speaking for ourselves, living, working, in which the voices and work of women are elevated, in which we are not just humanized, but even deified. This is the gist of the book I am currently writing.

As I have been blogging my thoughts on Pinay poetics, writing this essay, and thinking more about this book project, I have just heard from Tina Bartolome, a Pinay writer who is a San Francisco native, now finishing her MFA at Indiana University. I clicked over to her blog, and have found a treasure of thoughtful writing on her "literary universe," as a politicized Pinay writer. I appreciate and need this resonance; certainly, now as I write more and more about this Pinay "we" poetics, I want to be able to articulate clearly what storytelling can do. Here are some points Tina has outlined:

Storytelling as taking inventory

Storytelling as collective memory

Storytelling as paying homage

Storytelling as a comrade to social change (a conversation in progress)

She elaborates on the last point by quoting Martín Espada's *Zapata's Disciple*, "Any oppressive social condition, before it can be changed, must be named and condemned in words that persuade by stirring the emotions, awakening the senses. Thus, the need for the political imagination." And then further down in her post, Tina tells us she wants writing to "mess with hegemony."

I recall Hayan Charara's essay, "Animals: On the Role of the Poet in a Country at War," in *Perihelion*:

And while I don't believe that poems will keep bombs from falling on schools, or bullets from entering bodies, or tanks from rolling over houses, or men or women or children from being humiliated, poetry insists on the humanity of people, which violence steals away; and poems advocate the power of the imagination, which violence seeks to destroy. Poets change the world. I don't mean literally, though some try. I mean with words, with language, they take the many things of this world and make them new, and when we read poems, we know the world and its many things differently—it might not be a better or worse place than the one we live in—just different—but without the imagination, without poetry, I don't believe that the world as most of us know it would be tolerable.

This is messing with hegemony, to insist upon poetry as a humanizing project, through which we may imagine, envision something other than what we're given, and inspire others to do the same — to think, to speak, to write, and to act in ways other than what is officially sanctioned. This is storytelling as transformative experience. Imagine Pinays transformed in international perception from consenting, silenced, servicing bodies in commerce into dignified human beings in the world; this transformation is facilitated in large part by art, literature, and cultural productions that we create, centering the Pinay, and portraying ourselves as speaking and acting human beings exercising free will and demanding to be heard.

Concerning "activism," I fear I am abstract; poems will not, as Charara writes, "keep bombs from falling on schools, or bullets from entering bodies, or tanks from rolling over houses." Still, considering the silences and noise of our everyday lives, I want neither of these. I want and need something else. Pinays are capable of so much bravery, and I need to connect with other Pinays who are brave, emboldened, who have opinions about the world, about art, about cultural movements, who are willing to engage in civil public discourse about these things—not just "thumbs up," not just "like," not just link. I believe these are the beginnings of a Pinay "we" poetics that messes with hegemony.

October 12, 2011 Questions for Today

- Do Filipino American communities need Filipino American literature? Why/why not?
- What do Filipino American communities need from Filipino American Literature?
- Is what they need the same as what they want?
- If not, as Filipino American authors, is that OK with you?
- As Filipino American authors, do you care about what Filipino American communities need and/or want?
- And if you care, how do you see your work in relation to what Filipino American communities need and/or want?

I am asking these questions, thinking again on the role of the artist in his/her communities, and certainly, in larger society: Represent? And what does it mean to represent? What specifically does it entail? To reflect, direct, affirm, educate, challenge, assuage, coddle, pander, anesthetize, indict, distract?

June 24, 2012 Manuscript Progress Report: On Anger, Rage, and Outrage

I have recently written here that I am struggling with my current manuscript, which I'm thinking of calling *She is a Picture of Magnificence*, after Estrella D. Alfon's short story, "Magnificence." The crux of my struggle is that while I have fashioned some very lovely poetry from approximately 20 different Fil Am women/Pinays who responded to a set of very open-ended questions, I found that the anger, rage, and outrage with which I have been accustomed to writing has been absent.

Surely, much of this has to do with how each of us individually expresses rage and outrage. These differences in expression have to do with aesthetics, with life experience, with how one prioritizes.

Viet Thanh Nguyen has just written on the uses of rage and anger in our work, over at the diacritics website. He asks, "What's the proper proportion of art to anger?" He acknowledges that we have a lot to be angry about/enraged at, as writers and artists from Southeast Asia:

> ...whether it's on the vast geopolitical/historical scale of
> countries and warfare and colonialism or whether it's on the
> much more intimate scale of families and love or the lack of
> love or the loss of love and so many other things. Even on the
> intimate scale, though, the horizon lines go directly to the
> macro-history of all the screwed up decisions and events that
> shaped us.

Still, I can see why anyone would not want to prioritize anger, rage, outrage in their own work. There's so much ugly shit out there in our own backyards, in our cushy suburbs, before we even get looking at the rest of the world. It can be overwhelming, even paralyzing. I understand the logic behind wanting to write the opposite of those ugly things, and while I understand, I don't necessarily agree. I believe we must continually write through the ugliness and horror; I also believe it will not realistically pass like a kidney stone anytime soon.

For myself, one of the major driving forces in my writing *Poeta en San Francisco* was (out)rage, and the process of writing that book was not just unpleasant, it was dark, intense, emotionally draining. It was a prolonged pit in the stomach. As M. Evelina Galang discusses in her continued hearing and writing of the Lolas' (Filipina "Comfort Women") narratives, I too had to learn to take care of myself. I then thought I would "take it easy" in writing *Diwata*, a celebration of the woman storyteller voice/persona and its historical persistence, but those glimmers of horror — immolation, dismemberment, abduction, rape, gang rape — came creeping into the text. I didn't stop it. I became more disturbed by my ability to write these things in such lovely poems. I also wrote war and porn, and the conflation of the two, in a series of poems, many of which became the chapbook *Cherry*. I wrote those poems until I was sick.

Sexual violence, especially when compounded by race, by religion, by foreign policy, remains a major fixture in my work.

I understand why many Pinays want some safe distance between me and them.

But I also have to say, when I hear other Pinays express self-doubt, wonder aloud whether what they have to say is important enough to write down, I want to ask, what are you not doing enough of to think what you have to say is not important? What are you not risking — is what you are writing not eating you up or not frightening you? Why aren't you writing stuff that if you don't get it out of your body, you will be so sick with it, you won't be able to stand it?

Or have you been led to believe (and by whom) that beautiful and clever language and turns of phrase and well-constructed narrative arcs suffice?

They don't.

I want to say, you have to be brave, and more brave still. I return to Audre Lorde's *The Cancer Diaries*, in which she writes about her own mortality, and the fact that if she did not speak her piece now, if she continued to wait to speak, then she would die having never spoken. She asks, must we all wait until we are dying to feel the urgency to speak? I ask that as well, because I don't want to wait until I am dying, to speak my mind.

So, I don't have an answer to Viet Nguyen's question, "What's the proper proportion of art to anger?" I want to respond by asking more questions. Why is being angry looked upon disdainfully, with shame? Is this our proper Filipina upbringing as las dalagas, as María Claras, that has disabled us from speaking our anger, or that has sanitized our ability to communicate that anger with honesty? If so, then we need to throw that upbringing in the basura; it serves to keep us acquiescent, to perpetuate Pinay victimhood — helplessness, silence, dependence, passivity. We Pinays cannot live in this world without (out)rage. Too much very real horrific shit happens to Pinay/WOC bodies to think we are ever truly safe from harm. To pretend we are safe does not make us safe.

So I return again to Alfon's beautiful story, "Magnificence," in which a Filipina mother handles with quiet efficiency the sexual predator that has been welcomed into her own home, that has invaded her and her children's safe space. (Remember the video from 1997, recorded by a person on a whale watching tour to the Farallones of the mother orca thrashing the great white shark that came to prey upon the orca baby? It was kind of like that.).

October 24, 2012 Women's Work as Guerrilla Fighters, Shipbuilders, Truth Tellers, Dominant Paradigm Subverters

I think of the literature I teach as neither specifically Filipino American, nor as Philippine Literature. I think of it as Filipinos in the World literature, for even as some specific subject matter may be of Filipino/a concern, I focus on themes with implications for larger communities of human beings — war, gender, self-determination.

Colonel Yay Panlilio's autobiography *The Crucible* is set in WWII in the Philippines. During this time, she had become a guerrilla camp commander. Panlilio's autobiography was originally published in the USA in 1950. Evangeline Buell writes non-fiction as well, and in the chapter "Grandma as Rosie the Riveter," in her memoir, *Twenty Five Chickens and a Pig for a Bride*, she tells the story of her grandmother who found war industry employment in the Richmond Shipyards. Buell's book was published in 2006. Between these two Filipino women authors who wrote from two different continents, half a century has passed. What their narratives have in common is this: both Yay Panlilio and Grandma Roberta were Filipina women, mothers in a time of war. Both asked questions about their own usefulness, about what could be their own meaningful contributions and work for the war effort. Both women made a decision to take action and assume traditionally non-feminine roles, and this very much changed their families.

Their questions, their actions speak against the dominant paradigm of women in war as passive, victimized, without agency, without voice, without the capability to make decisions, and whose contributions are either non-existent or peripheral to what men give, what men decide, and what men execute. Women's contributions in war therefore, are acts of more broadly defined individual and collective heroism as workers and leaders, and which serve to question and decenter the singular importance of the American savior (of the Filipino, of the Philippines, of the world).

Yay Panlilio's narrative underscores the contributions of women (American and Filipina, as she was both), and the contributions of the guerrilla fighters. Her narrative strategies are multi-layered and seem contradictory then; she praises the Americans for their generosity and ideals of freedom and democracy, but centers her text around the guerrilla fighters, who fought for those ideals, but held as a priority their own people's safety and liberation. Her ultimate message is that neither women nor Filipinos in the war were without agency, and even with eventual access to advanced and abundant American weaponry, these guerrillas were the heart of the fight. And she led them. These are not my own original ideas here; I owe a debt of gratitude to Denise Cruz for bringing Yay Panlilio's writing back into print, and for her wonderful introduction to the new volume which was published by Rutgers University Press in 2010.

Panlilio's narrative also utilizes the theme of motherhood throughout; this also seems to be a strategy. In assuming a role not traditionally female, she expands upon our social expectations of mothers. In the guerrilla camp, she is the soldiers' and General Marcos (Marking) V.

Augustin's emotional center and emotional backbone. Yes, this could also be a female stereotype, but consider that the emotional centers and backbones of a community or family are the leaders who keep their constituents in check, and call them out when they're not acting right, and this is what she did, as a daily practice for three years in the jungle. As their emotional backbone, she earned their respect as a decision maker and strategist.

Buell's Grandma Roberta is also an active agent exercising self-determination, in finding war industry employment and becoming a dual-income household, as an immigrant and limited English speaker conquering her previous fears of leaving the house to encounter the racist American world outside her door; she becomes emboldened to contribute meaningfully to the household decision making and in enforcing rules, rather than deferring to her spouse. Because of her employment, she is no longer the full-time housewife, and her spouse must now agree to share homemaking responsibilities with her.

I want to add to these women's WWII narratives Ruth Elynia Mabanglo's persona poem, "Ballad of Lola Amonita" (which is the English translation of her original Tagalog "Balada ni Lola Amonita"), and M. Evelina Galang's nonfiction work in progress, *Lola's House: Women Living With War*. These are "Comfort Woman" narratives, which I do not read or teach as victim narratives. Think of Mabanglo's poem as providing testimony; "Comfort Women" did not speak of their experiences for 50 years, half a century of imposed silences, for the benefit of others, to spare or protect others from shame. In Mabanglo's poem, the young Amonita sees her father ashamed that he could not protect her. She knows that her mother and grandmother cannot reconcile the girl's new impurity with their religious faith.

Now, this half a century of silence has erased the Lolas from history books' official version of the war, and has allowed the Japanese government to disavow the systematized atrocities of their imperial army against the women and girls of the nations they occupied and brutalized. Mabanglo's poem is a survivor's narrative, the beginning of the truth telling, after which comes the examination of evidence, after which comes the verdict.

The Lolas about whom Galang writes assert that they will tell their stories again and again, as many times as necessary, no matter how painful, even though they relive their experiences of rape and abduction every time they speak. They must tell their stories in order to protect the following generations of Filipinas. That's us. The Lolas demand historical inclusion and proper compensation. The Lolas demand a formal apology. These are women whom history would brand as victims. So then, not only are these survivor narratives. These are Filipina lists of grievances and demands.

I will end with Yay Panlilio: "I wrote into my column advice for the women: 'Let your children look back and remember how their mothers faced the war'." "How they faced," or, "how they confronted." So in the conventionally feminine realm of the advice column, she subverts the reader's expectation of fluff and domesticity, and makes a profound statement about women's capabilities.

October 26, 2012 Women's Work: Mentoring and Professor-ing

Just so this is clear: The work I do is not mothering. This needs to be explicitly stated because it is the implicit expectation when we come into positions in which we are required to be knowledgeable, to be leaders, to be teachers. I suspect that expectation for us to mother is about the need for a quick and easy boxing/categorization of us, rather than challenging the dominant narrative that all women's work must be reproductive work, nurturing work rooted in private spaces/domesticity, unrecognized (invisible) emotional maintenance work, in which reproductive work is always subordinate to productive work.

I am thinking of Annie Finch's "Women Poets & Mentoring" essay at the Poetry Foundation's Harriet blog, how women claim to not have been mentored by other women, and how women omit mention of their women mentors, and therefore erase their women mentors. How do we create lineages when we are so engaged in erasure.

Within a Pinayist context (as Pinayist criticism), there is the belief that we must debunk that there can be only one of us in the public eye. This belief necessitates erasure and marginalization of women, women of color, immigrant women; in our powerlessness, we instead turn against one another and fight among ourselves for that perceived one spot. As Dawn Bohulano Mabalon stated critically in Allyson Tintiangco-Cubales's "Pinayism" essay in *Pinay Power: Peminist Critical Theory,* "Because there can only be one Jessica [Hagedorn], because there can be only one beauty queen. ... Because there was only one María Clara." There is no "sisterhood," camaraderie, or community in this situation, but gangs of playground mean girls making drama and tsismis. Nor is there space for focused discussion of production, professional needs and outcomes. Production and productiveness are stunted and sidelined. Needs and outcomes become about providing (uncompensated) emotional maintenance, and oneupmanship (Unseating "the one"? Is that success? By whose standards?). Emotional maintenance is reproductive work. And there we are again at that gendered expectation.

I return to mentoring, how I was mentored and by whom. Women literary mentors in my life have come to me from different places, whether or not I actively sought them out (did I even know to seek them out) when I was a student and emerging poet. Cristina Pantoja Hidalgo taught me Filipina Literature at UP Diliman. Elizabeth Treadwell opened up my poetics during the one semester as my community college creative writing instructor, and turned me towards grad school. Eileen Tabios advised me as the editor of my first poetry collection and taught me how to navigate and negotiate literary spaces as a Filipina. Stacy Doris saw me through numerous graduate writing workshops, served as my thesis advisor, and opened up multilingualism and translation for me. Women who provided me concrete opportunities as editors include Luisa Igloria, Marianne Villanueva, Summi Kaipa. Women whose narratives, whose relative proximity enabled me to envision possibility and create my own opportunities include Jessica Hagedorn, Ninotchka Rosca, Shirley Ancheta, Vangie Buell, Catalina Cariaga. And now those who continue to provide concrete support, in the form of teaching, endorsing, reviewing include Evelina Galang, Elmaz Abinader, Juliana Spahr.

As an author, as a teacher and mentor, I want the work in the foreground, not the demand of mothering. One of my mentors told me years ago that she advises her students to keep their "emotional hygiene" in check, and this term is helpful for me.

As a teacher of Pinay Literature, I am most interested in discussing works by women writers whose speakers and characters question and critically engage their gendered circumstances, whether or not they can truly subvert those gendered circumstances. The critical questioning is where it begins; how aware are they, and how deeply entrenched? What would meaningful subversion be/look like? Is it feasible? What are the consequences of transgression? Who defines transgression? Who polices, who enforces, who punishes?

As a mentor of women and Pinay writers, especially when some poetic projects do necessarily come from deep emotional places, how to provide clarity, guidance, and support for writers as their projects develop, take shape, and grow, while maintaining my own personal and professional boundaries.

As a working author who is Pinay, how to impart the importance of a work ethic and the fact that there is a process and industry about which we must be knowledgeable, so that we may enter into it empowered and focused, able to prioritize and make decisions about publication and distribution.

So then, mentorship that is feminist, womanist, Pinayist — what does this look like? How may it be enacted?

July 3, 2013 Progress, Perigee: Some notes I've made

So here's something else I've been thinking about manuscript progress — order, trajectory, the shape of the thing. I don't think that linear is appropriate for what I am trying to convey; clean progression or emergence from darkness into light, from oppression, suppression, repression into freedom of speech and action would not really work here. That's too tidy and simple, and it doesn't work that way in real life. I'm thinking of the spiderweb structure of *Diwata*, how does this help me now as I'm constructing this current series of cyclical regression/progression, internal dialogue/external speech, domestic space/outside world, sanctioned/unsanctioned spaces, tradition abiding/tradition transgressing, memory and dream/here and now/ future looking.

- Women/Pinays in spaces other than domestic spaces. Can we think of our places not just the kitchen, and the nuclear family home.
- Women/Pinays in traditionally male spaces.
- Women/Pinays articulate in public, traditionally male spaces.
- Women/Pinays not curio objects, not spectacle.
- Women/Pinays acting in ways dictated as traditionally male. Not seeking the approval and permission of others. Outspoken. Ambitious. Leaders. Intellectuals. Disobedient. Physically strong. Confident. Libidinous. Unaccommodating. All of these not as aberration/exception.
- Women/Pinays encouraging one another, fostering space in order to be/do as listed above, versus policing one another to prevent, discourage these qualities.
- All of the above exacerbated by race and ethnicity.

So it's a constant movement and struggle. One Pinay speaks and is silenced by others. One Pinay advances, and others beg or force her to retreat. One Pinay advances and is intimidated into retreating. One Pinay advances, tries to bring others with her, and those others retreat. This movement, a planet in retrograde.

March 10, 2014 I am a Filipino American Writer in the Hustle and I Love the Book

Many movements. Many targets.

I have written extensively about Filipino American literature, and the "hustle" in which we participate. For many of us, it is a matter of necessity. Some things that brew up in my classrooms full of young Filipino Americans, many of whom are reading Filipino/Fil Am Lit for the first time: First is the more obvious question of, "Where have these books been my entire life; my parents, my teachers never told me about these." Then, "Wow, look what these Filipinos are capable of," and then, "Wow, I think I can also be capable of this."

I tell people all the time that picking up Jessica Hagedorn's *Dogeaters* when I was a freshman at UC Berkeley was life changing. There was my personal journal, a hardbound book with a glossy, blue marble cover. Its pages were edged with gold. I wrote in this book with a Waterman fountain pen. My penmanship was impeccable. My poems were private.

I found *Maganda* magazine that year too. Or, *Maganda*'s Ray Orquiola found me, invited me to share my poems. I was ecstatic and terrified. That was my first poetry reading; it was 1990, and I was 19. *Maganda* published my poems. Then *Liwanag II* in the mid-1990s. After this, I didn't know where else to go. After graduating from college and taking Elizabeth Treadwell's Creative Writing class at Berkeley City College, I made my first poetry portfolio, and then I made my first Kinko's DIY chapbook. Elizabeth recommended I go to grad school. I did. While I was in grad school, Marie Romero of Arkipelago Books proposed I submit a poetry manuscript to her, and suggested Eileen Tabios be my editor. That was my first book, *Gravities of Center*, published in 2003.

I committed to submitting poems to various literary journals. Then, online journals were so new, questions always arose whether that was considered "legitimate publication." Remember Jim Behrle's canwehaveourballback.com, and Del Ray Cross's *Shampoo Poetry* website. Vince Gotera, creator of our international Filipino writers listserv, who was also the editor of *North American Review*, published one of my poems, and gave me my first Pushcart nomination. I always thought that people who published me and offered me opportunities did so because they were being nice.

For my MFA thesis, I worked with Stacy Doris, who was an immense mentor and critic, well-capable of reading multilingual, postcolonial, feminist text. I submitted my thesis, which I titled *Poeta en San Francisco*, to Susan Schultz at TinFish Press (I'd been asking for suggestions for publishers, and poets Shin Yu Pai and Paolo Javier said TinFish would be a good fit). While searching for funding sources to cover printing costs, I won the James Laughlin Award of the Academy of American Poets. Our original idea for a print run was 750. This first print run was increased to 5000 for the Academy, and 2000 more for TinFish. A couple of years later, we had a second print run of 2000.

I have visited classes as a guest writer; I've brought my own DIY chapbooks to give away to students. I have done readings in local community venues, and brought my own DIY chapbooks to raise funds for these venues. The poems, or series of poems that didn't fit into my three full length collections became the three chapbooks, *Easter Sunday*, *Cherry*, and *For the City That Nearly Broke Me*. I love chapbooks, and believe in them as their own compact and powerful bodies, each with its own focused reach.

I offer this quickie recap of my publication history to illustrate the many places I have chosen to publish. I choose different paths, different venues, reaching many different populations of readers. Now that I teach, I am always looking in so many places for different kinds of work, each with its own ideas of reach. There are all kinds of amazing narratives in our community, writers so hungry to be heard, read, and seen, who want so badly to get their books into the world, to be recognized for their work.

I want to amplify our own. Our narratives are great. Some of our authors are Fucking Bad Ass. We are not silent (reticent, fearful, unambitious), and we are not invisible (hiding, hidden). There is no reason why we shouldn't aspire to greatness, and given that we spend so much time in the margins, to position ourselves front and center.

I advocate for publishing books in the big world. There is no reason why we shouldn't want the narratives of our community widely distributed and disseminated, to find all the Filipinos who are trying to find us.

Finally, I Love the Book. I became a writer because of this Love. I cannot force anyone to Love the Book, the way I Love the Book. But I do want them to experience the Book, and not fear the Book. As critical readers, we can manage and understand many Books. Maybe our Books can plant the seed in them, that they can also be capable of writing Books. When young people tell me that reading *Poeta en San Francisco* made all the difference to them, as readers, as emerging writers themselves, trying to find their way and willing to work hard, I think of this wonderful continuity, and am glad that I have contributed to enlarging the space where Filipino Americans can envision themselves as authors, work to create kick ass writing, and make their authordom happen.

January 26, 2016 On Grit and the Burden of Representation

Is my work really that brutal? And if it is brutal, what specifically is so brutal about/in it? And then, is that a bad thing? I continually ask these questions, as I ask myself whether I want my poetry to "do" anything, to serve some kind of purpose, and what kind of purpose.

I've been reading essays about this burden of representation that is thrust upon the work of POC writers. I think this is a problem. Who wants us to represent, what do they want us to represent, why do they want us to represent in the ways that they want us to represent. Within our own communities, this preference for the positive, uplifting, beautiful portraits and narratives of us. How we look when we are well dressed. How we look when we are acting "right," and "proper," when things go our way, which I think of as a reaction against the centuries of "negative" portrayals of us. But then we have to think about whose value systems determine "negative," "positive," "beautiful." I question whether the beautiful and uplifting portraits and narratives are honest and realistic ones.

Beauty, positivity are things we talk about in my classes especially when we read Jessica Hagedorn's *Dogeaters*. How do we respond to these "ugly" people doing "ugly" things to one another. How do we feel that these "ugly" people are Filipino, and that they are each "ugly" in various, multiple ways. Why write about these people and this society and centralize their ugliness? These days, my students are so young, mostly second and third generation Americans with much distance from Philippine society, from the original publication and original brouhahas, that they generally don't take it personally that Hagedorn's characters are so "ugly," and that Philippine society is portrayed as this "ugly" thing. So then we can talk about how this ugliness came to be. Also, by the time we get to the *Dogeaters* portion of the syllabus, we've already been talking intensely about colonialism, class and privilege, about the violence and criminalization of poverty of Filipinos in both the Philippines and the US West Coast in Bulosan's *The Laughter of My Father* and *America is in the Heart*. So we already know our histories are not pretty.

I bring these things up because I feel like we have blinders on as a community. Are we still trying so hard to pretend no one writes about the terrible things that have befallen us in the world; glossing over all the desperation, hunger, assault, and institutional violence in Bulosan, to talk about cultural pride; forgetting that a novel that takes place during wartime such as Tess Uriza Holthe's *When the Elephants Dance* takes place when the country was getting the hell bombed out of it, when women and girls were being abducted and forced into sex slavery, when people were starving, their homes destroyed; forgetting when we are reading Mia Alvar's *In the Country*, that Filipino domestic workers in the Middle East are being violated of their human rights on the regular, and abused as property/replaceable objects. Weird dissociations.

Our literature is about how we suffer, work, cope, survive, get gritty and fight, persevere, and celebrate. Then get back to work again. And so this is cyclical, ongoing, because this literature exists in the real world, written by real, working people who live in the real gritty, brutal world.

What if we — the diasporic Filipino writer and reader — fundamentally disagree on what literature is supposed to do; not all writers agree on what our work is supposed to do, and if it's supposed to do anything at all. I think of writing and literature as mirror, as microscope, as archeological dig. I think also of spell casting, committing to the page the words for what you would like to manifest. But before we get to that, as we are digging, we don't know what exactly we are going to unearth, and so what happens when the "problem" and/or premise gets bigger and more complicated, monstrous, personal and social, historical and contemporary. The process becomes complicated. The spell casting becomes complicated too. What do I really want to make manifest? There are no easy remedies, no band-aids, no neatly tied up packages. Rewards are hard to come by, and can be fleeting. My idea of reward may not be your idea of reward. What comes next? Are we done? Everything is all good now? We've made it? I don't think so. So then I write the next thing, dig through the next heap of shit towards hopefully something awesome. Sometimes I just keep on unearthing shit, and what to do with it all.

That is my experience as a writer. What if the reader, what if the community wants something else, remedies and band-aids and neatly tied up packages? *Life is hard. Life as a brown person in the USA is hard. Is there any escape? Can you please give it a rest and give me my escapism? And/or: Filipinos always get a bad rap. Can you please use your power for good? No more maids, mail order brides, drug mules, gang members, wife beaters, and swindlers. Can you please write something that will give our youth pride and self-esteem? Something that tells the world how beautiful we are? You're really more of an American anyway, so what do you know; your version of Filipino is inauthentic because it does not mirror mine. Therefore, you are a fake Filipino. You write in proper English, you publish with white publishers, therefore, you are writing for white people, and you are not down with your own community; you are a whitewashed, colonized Filipino who is really an American who doesn't know and doesn't care about what it's really like to be Filipino.*

And what about the burden of representation that comes from outside our communities — *tell us what the real, genuine, authentic Filipino is. Tell us all about your victimhood and trauma as an oppressed and colonized people. Give us all the details of your patriarchal suffering. How were you violated, and how did you feel, being violated. Leave none of the pain out. You have to make us understand everything, so you must translate all your foreign words and you must explain everything that is ethnic and alien. It's your job to make us understand, and if we don't understand, then it's your fault, and your work is deficient.*

So that's where I'm currently at. Somewhere in this bullshit is me, just wanting to write poems. I would like to think I am writing about important things. But to be a writer who is a woman and a Filipino in this country can be strange. For now, all I can say is that I choose to stay gritty and not be bullied by any demographic so much that their demands take precedence over what and how I mean to write, as I continually work to figure out what and how that is.

August 8, 2016 Myth: Reading Others Will Compromise Your Own "Authentic" Voice

Seriously, where does this myth come from, and why is it perpetuated, and by whom.

I've heard it said, in actual public events, by aspiring writers, who say, "I don't read anyone; I don't want anyone to influence my voice." Perhaps you will tell me that "aspiring" is the key word in the above sentence. I think you're right.

I do know that when you are in a writing workshop, you (1) are reading so many other people's works, and (2) have a workshop leader or teacher assigning you readings by other writers, creating writing assignments out of these.

While I was in community college writing workshop with Elizabeth Treadwell as my teacher, and with Michelle Bautista and Lupe Ortiz as my classmates, so much discussion and reading outside of my own context enabled me to get started writing what became my first book, *Gravities of Center*. My mentors Eileen Tabios and Jaime Jacinto were constantly feeding me stimuli, giving me reading recommendations and introductions to poetic voices so different from my own; they asked me hard questions, how to use the page, how to make density or white space do what I want it to do, and do things I could not have foreseen, how to be open to these new things. That is how I finished writing my first book.

In grad school, Stacy Doris had us writing poems in the voices/styles of our colleagues. She also had us come up with recommended readings for our colleagues, based upon what we'd read of their manuscripts in progress. Building root systems from which a number of my poems in *Poeta en San Francisco* and *Diwata* came to grow — it was good to get out of my own head and out of my own voice to try something else, to find something in someone else's voice that becomes the big Eureka moment, to find pieces of that other person's voice that could aid me in tweaking my own process, if even just slightly. Sometimes that's all we need at that moment, not a hard shove but a nudge.

This is another way, a more concrete way of discussing poetry community for me. This happened again at Kuwentuhan, where we were riffing off one another's works as a regular practice, sitting together at a big table, sharing Tanduay Rhum and food, sharing writing prompts, sharing drafts, sharing so much. I finished writing *Invocation to Daughters* because of Kuwentuhan. Those poems about grieving for my dad, I really could not have written on my own, as I was so deep in my own sadness and just couldn't do much of anything, my life and my head were turned so upside-down.

During Kuwentuhan, I had a conversation with a fellow author about how movements are born, from communities just doing their thing. And that's really all it is. A bunch of us getting together and doing our thing. You can get with or create an arts org, and you can get together with artists you know, and you can just do your thing together, which ultimately means inspiring one another to make art.

So, those who wish not to be influenced by other artists. I don't get it. I don't see the benefit of it. I see only the kind of stuff that makes you mad and counterproductive. That alone feeling that makes you feel like you have absolutely no idea where to start, no one who understands where you are coming from, no one who will ever read your work. There's no reason to have any of that.

September 28, 2016 Kuwentuhan: Event, Scene, Thing, Publication

We wanted to make a Thing. Some kind of Event, involving writers in Live (or living) space.

Some background: I am a writer, and I am a cheerleader of publishing and publication. I believe in that as evidence, as document. I love the book. I don't have real specific bookmaking vocabulary, but I love the book as a thing I write, that finds itself into the world in the hands of readers who might look like me, who might be looking for work by someone who looks like them. I love the smell of the paper pages, the weight of the cover stock. The perfect bind. Lovely cover design. Clean typography.

I get a lot of questions from aspiring authors who just don't want to go through the whole manuscript submissions process/rigmarole. They have different reasons. Sometimes it's about timeliness; they don't want to wait for a time slot on an editorial calendar. Sometimes it's political; they don't want to submit themselves to what they have come to believe is a capitalist process in which we writers and the fruits of our labor are treated as someone else's commodities. Most of the time, it's about fear and lack of knowledge of what the process entails and how it works. They don't know they have to find presses and editors that would be open to their politics, aesthetics, and themes. They don't know about open reading periods or cover letters. They fear rejection as an absolute assessment of their worth. They are already discouraged by how much work it is before they have even begun. They already believe that all editors are white, and that all white editors would not understand and appreciate where we writers of color are coming from.

At the most recent Filipino American International Book Festival, an older man who I'd never met before, who self-published his tome, demanded I tell him whether he made a mistake self-publishing. Then before I had an opportunity to fully process the question, he proceeded to explain to me why he decided to go the route he did, and what he believed the benefits were. Most of these benefits were monetary; every cent earned goes back to him. He didn't mention design, though from what I saw, he could have benefited from having a designer. He didn't mention editing, though with a tome, I generally believe some paring down can only strengthen a written work. He didn't mention distribution, book reviews, or libraries. He didn't mention course adoption. Not to say all books succeed only with course adoption. But books — our works — do need to move from our brains into readers' hands.

I get a lot of questions from new authors about how to connect with readers. I have no magic formula or special knowledge on this. I do know it's important to ask who and where readers are.

I write all this now, thinking about Kuwentuhan, being based in lived experience, now something I must figure out a way to write. One poem that came directly from our Kuwentuhan table will be in my next book, *Invocation to Daughters*. It's a five page prose poem called, "The Day" — the best way I can describe it is that its central focus is my dad, and how no matter what I do on a daily basis, in routine, in the city, online, internally, socially, I continually circle back to my memories of him and the day he passed away. There's linear time, and that's how the poem is structured; and then there's the cycling back I and we do, how and what we remember.

So this is what I started thinking about as Angela Narciso Torres provided 24-hour poem writing prompts to us at the Kuwentuhan table. I couldn't separate the banal from the profound, and I think that's the point. Not that I must write about every grilled cheese sandwich I eat, or what shoes I am wearing today, or every lipstick color that ends up on a palette on the back of my hand at Sephora, but that I go deep into the details of my dailiness, locate the things I am really thinking about, and then be open to mining those. And to allow myself to still be surprised. In many ways, it's re-calibrating my filters. I know I go through cycles of really tightening my filters, super-efficient sorting and chucking, and then I need to loosen up, open up again, give myself actual reflection time.

This poetic loosening happened to me another time, long time ago at the Poetry Center at SFSU, with Al Robles and Lawson Fusao Inada whose poems and poetic practices demonstrated an openness which structured writing programs can sometimes shut. After an afternoon of just basking in their presences, I opened my notebook and wrote like crazy, everything, in every corner of my neighborhood, my commute, my every glass of whiskey. So then about structures of time again, and recurrence.

One thing I am coming away with for now, is the challenge of conveying these ideas in poems, in books of poems. Can the book ever truly give you, dear reader, even a smidgen of the complex sets of emotions and realizations, the rapid fire connections that happen in real time, in lived experience, in amazing conversations and interactions with others.

I want to believe it can. This is why I persist with writing and publishing. I don't want there to be a divide between "publishing culture," and "the stage," "the event," the "you just had to be there." Because what if you weren't? Through no fault of your own, you weren't there. I don't want this to exclude you from what could be a great, revelatory process. And there's a contradiction too, the lived event supposed to be more inclusive, but "you just had to be there" as exclusionary — "if you weren't there, then you just wouldn't understand."

The publication travels, transcends linear time, finds itself in the hands of readers the author could not have completely foreseen. Years later, decades later. We're still talking about Rizal, Bulosan, and Villa, aren't we. So there's memory, there's stories of folks who were there or knew someone who knew someone, and then there are the widely circulated/distributed "Mi Último Adiós," *Noli Mi Tangere*, "If You Want to Know What We Are," *America is in the Heart, Doveglion*. And all of these things together are important.

All this to say, I must write more about Kuwentuhan. I must write more to my fellow Kuwentuhan authors Arlene Biala, Javier O. Huerta, Urayoán Noel, Aimee Suzara, Lehua M. Taitano, and Angela Narciso Torres. Urayoán Noel wrote, "Party Like It's 1898!" over at the Poetry Foundation, "Looking back on how much fun I had at Kuwentuhan, and how close I felt to my fellow poets, I realized we were all working in one way or another on decolonial poetics, and we were also all in some sense children of 1898." I want more spaces and events like this, more interactions with poets like this, historically critical, willing to be playful, emotionally honest, experimental, prolific. I want to write and mail more handwritten letters to poets, shout poetry through megaphones to people in the streets, tell story around large tables full of Filipino food.

May 9, 2017 For #APIAHeritageMonth, Considering my Fil Am Immigrant Family History

It feels more than appropriate to begin this #APIAHeritageMonth post by saying, "Yes, my parents were right." Of course they were right. I was too young and stubborn to listen to them, until I wasn't.

By "right," this is what I mean. When I was in college, I was floundering. UC Berkeley was challenging, and though I was as academically prepared as I could be, having been on the honors and AP track in my Catholic college prep high school, I wasn't emotionally ready, and I wasn't mature enough yet to be self-motivated and accountable, and I wasn't disciplined enough yet to be on my own.

I resented my parents for stressing their hard work ethic, their grind, and their ideas of success. I thought of myself as a rebel. I saw what my American classmates had, conversational, casual, chummy relationships with their apparently easy-going and permissive parents. My classmates had what I saw as leisure time and super chill parents who would ask them how they were feeling, and who would talk about art.

I had a perpetually stressed out mother, who worked full time and managed to raise four of us, and a father so uptight, I thought he'd bust an aneurysm when he was in his 40s. They didn't seem to want to understand "American" ways, all the things I thought were cool about how my friends could behave and speak in their parents' homes. They talked about their feelings; my parents didn't have time for that. My father would get so indignant if we ever used American slang/idiom when directly addressing him. When I was young, I could never imagine ever telling him to chill out, or not to have a cow. Answering back always erupted into WWIII; he wasn't into my American sass mouth one bit.

I felt like nothing I ever did was good enough. They always wanted me to do more. I hated this. Yes, sometimes I rebelled. Sometimes I tried. I failed a lot. I hated this. I always thought American parents were more understanding of failure. That they would just say, it's OK, honey. Just try again.

And when I was in college, living far enough away from my parents for the first time ever, I couldn't discipline myself to get to an 11 am class on time. I got a D in calculus (why the hell was I even taking calculus anyway). I had the worst GPA ever. I stopped showing up to class altogether. I wasted a ton of time and money. I couch surfed a lot, having no desire to move back home, nor the means to pay rent. I wrote poetry. And some of my friends thought I was pretty badass — today, they still talk about the free spirit they saw in me then. It was romantic. And it was unsustainable.

My parents finally left me alone, and it was cool, because then I could just work my crappy part time job, write, party, smoke, and drink. And I thought it was such an edgy, rebellious life of struggling to pay rent, being an artist, and scraping up nickels with my friends to afford to split $2 nachos in the student union. And my parents let me be, until they couldn't.

They wanted to know what the hell I was doing with my life. I evaded them, wouldn't come home for weeks at a time. When I did see them, I could see the disappointment in their body language. I was a failure to them. I was always broke. I was a dropout. But I was writing poems! And I was so cool on the mic! And I was living according to my own rules! Fuck the Man! Fuck the Establishment! This life of glorified, self-imposed artist poverty, screwing the system!

I thought they were so rigid, so old school, for thinking I was a failure, for thinking my ass should go back to college. I wanted to yell at them; I was following my dream! What the fuck did they know about dreams and romance!

Well. Here's where the gift of age, experience, and hindsight kick in.

What did my parents know about dreaming and romance? Didn't they leave everything behind, when they were in their early 20s. Didn't they get on an airplane, to come and live in a foreign country, on another continent. Didn't they know there were no guarantees. Didn't they know coming here to work, and to raise their children was a gamble, probably the riskiest thing they had ever done, and weren't they throwing caution to the wind as they did. Didn't all they have was an idea, a dream of what it might be like.

I am thinking of this old photograph, a colored photo of my young parents, with me and my older sister. I must have been about four. My sister would have been six. My parents would have been in their mid-20s. We are in Reno, at a motel, posed by the motel swimming pool. We are on a road trip. We are on a family vacation. This would have been two years after my sister and I immigrated. My parents had already come before us, found employment, saved money, and so by the time my sister and I were here, we moved from a Daly City one room apartment into our first home in Fremont, and my sister was enrolled in a private school.

Imagine the kind of courage that takes. My mother used to tell us that we had to work twice as hard as American kids did. I resented this and I resented her for saying it; I also knew it was true.

My younger sister, who is now an executive in a media company that turns these homemade snapshots into enormous, lasting historical documents, tells it like this (though she wasn't born yet), when she presents this image to company shareholders and clients: this image is important and historical because it documents the persistence of these two young immigrants, to make something out of nothing, to make a life here, for themselves and their children. How precious is this kind of vacation time. It's almost like a celebration of their "making it" here.

So then, yes, my parents did dream. They dreamed of a life. They made it happen. And here we are.

I thought about this a lot, during my father's last days. What kind of life did he lead here. Was it a meaningful life. Did he accomplish what he meant to accomplish in his life, which was one full of travel, and art, always surrounded by family, friends, and loved ones, always sharing what he had, always celebrating something in the most lively manner possible — this kind of wealth. While I miss him like crazy, what keeps me going is that, while our family has never been perfect, while we've all had our share of disappointments, and while we fought like hell, almost everything he and my mother wanted for us, we got, and we have.

At his wake, people I didn't know well at all, were coming up to me and my sisters, nodding with approval. To me, they would say, "Ah, so you're the professor," or "Ah, so you're the poet." This is how my father talked about us to his friends and relatives. And rather than make this about status (which I know some of you will want to do), let me just say that this is how proud he was of us. This is how he talked about us; he approved highly of the people we became after each of us found our own way — this was so important to him, that everybody knew it.

All of this to say — I have something in my eye — what my parents gave us transcends material things. My sisters and I worked to become what we wanted to become, to have gardens and celebrations, and time together with family, because this is the wealth we inherited from our parents. Most of all though, I think the best part is thinking about change, and malleability. That it happens in ways you can't always detect, but before you know it, you are doing things your way, and your hard ass traditional parents aren't so traditional anymore, and not having a cow about you being a poet, about being tattooed, about being a smart mouth. Or maybe they are still traditional, but now, because you are determined, doing things your way, the resulting achievements, and the fact that you are happy with your work and your life — these are what become most important to your traditional parents.

My first *Invocation to Daughters* event will take place on his two-year death anniversary, and it's bittersweet as all hell. Because this book is exactly what I wanted, and exactly what I worked for. And because of this, he would have approved. I also didn't know that his approval meant as much to me as it does.

November 10, 2017 Dear Poeta, Dear Pinay, Why Do You Want To Write Books?

I remember once, some years ago, I was part of a group of authors of color who came as guest speakers to Willie Perdomo's VONA Poetry class. A couple of the questions from students that I remember, and the discussions that stayed with me were as follows:

Why do you want to write books? Why is writing and having books published important to you? For me, my initial reaction was, why is this even a question? One of the other guest authors responded by saying, "because it's tradition." Yes, this made all the sense in the world to me then, and it continues to be one of my go-to responses. I did think hard about why this tradition is important to me. Here's my go at it:

As young people who think we have a knack for telling story, for composing verse, we inherit so much of this from our families. Maybe we have a particular "ear" for story, or sensitivity for where and how stories are being told in our families and by whom. We learn how to listen and ask.

I remember all my little notebooks full of ditties and rhymes. I don't remember if my keeping these notebooks was actively encouraged, but it was surely not discouraged. Regular visits to the library and the bookstore were definitely encouraged. We had some books in the house. Not really "high literature," but I don't think that part mattered so much. I just knew I came from a family who did read some books, and who did actively, enthusiastically make kuwento.

I started to feel simultaneously attracted and frustrated by canonical literature in middle school and high school. I don't know that I was feeling "pushed out" of the world of books and high literature, but I remember trying so hard to find ways in. I don't remember being particularly "good" at English class. I wanted to be an insightful reader, and to say deep, profound things about what I had read. I wasn't there yet.

And when, in college, I found myself immersed in literatures of folks of color, immigrants, feminists, indigenous communities, things really clicked. I started to understand. I learned to articulate those deep profound things I'd always wanted to. I wanted this. Whether it was books by Amy Tan, or Maxine Hong Kingston, or Leslie Marmon Silko, or Gloria Anzaldúa, or Jessica Hagedorn, or Carlos Bulosan, or Audre Lorde, I wanted that. I was hungry for that.

Tracing some of these authors' lineages brought me to The Beats, to Whitman, and so forth. And I was opened. I wanted that. When I finally connected with other aspiring and emerging writers of color, one thing we had in common was that hunger. We struggled to find our way into multiple literary worlds. Some of us struggled to better our craft.

The books I was reading became increasingly diverse, ethnically and aesthetically. I didn't know much about the publishing industry, but I did know what poetry books I was actively seeking out and drawn to — poets whose books were published by New Directions Publishers, poets in translation published by Copper Canyon Press, and the City Lights Pocket Poets. I also knew that a lot of my literary Manangs and Manongs were getting published by Kearny Street Workshop. When Jaime Jacinto's first book, *Heaven is Just Another Country* was published, I was there on the mic, a young college dropout serving as guest poet dropping some spoken word, thinking, I too could one day do what Jaime had just done.

When I was selling my first Kinko's produced DIY chapbook out of my backpack at Bindlestiff Studio, before I ever went to grad school, Jaime Jacinto, Eileen Tabios, and Marianne Villanueva were there to receive it and to encourage me to keep at it.

A few years ago, I was in Seattle, and Jon Pineda and I were finding our way to a Seattle Filipino American community literary event. We were talking about what our publishing prospects were, and I told him about City Lights. We both said, they published *Howl*. And then we both said, *whoa*, and *aw shit*. Though, today, I would also say, they published Juan Felipe Herrera. They published Diane di Prima's *Revolutionary Letters*. They published Anne Waldman's *Fast Speaking Woman*. They are here, in San Francisco, the place which has defined me and my poetic voice and political values, and the city whose shadow I always felt concealed me. Right next to Manilatown. Boom. I am telling you where I would like to place myself in literary tradition.

Wanting to become a writer of books has everything to do with tradition. And everything to do with our love for the object called the book. Its thick card stock matte covers and thick off-white, cream stock interior pages, super clean typography, spines' perfect binding.

Keepsakes. Gifts. You always take them with you.

My home is filled with them. My ceilings are so high, and my walls are entirely covered with book shelves.

I was educated by veterans of the Third World Liberation Front, mentored by Kearny Street Workshop elders. I have made my home where the Black Panthers were birthed. I am here, in Oakland, working for the health of a growing, changing Chinatown community, especially its children, girls, and women. I am educating young Pinays to find their voices, and not to be afraid of how capable they are of working towards social change. I am here, seeing their eyes

and smiles widen, their bodies stand tall, when I put a Pinay
authored book in their hands.

All of this is why I am an author of books.

May 10, 2018 #APIAHeritageMonth #APAHM: How women hustle against erasure

Barbara Jane Reyes
1 hr · 🌐 ▾

I am finally working on revisions on my essay re: Asian American Literature.
And as I talk about how my undergrads really don't care who's MFA'ed and
awarded and who's a darling to which canon-making institution, I am thinking
about, questioning my own impulse to publish/be published consistently.

I wish I were more chill -- I see people who've got a book or two, who seem to
be living their lives entirely outside of the industry just fine. And sometimes I
envy that, wish I could just drop out of it. It's an ego thing holding me back from
actually doing what I regularly threaten to do. Why do I need recognition.
Whose recognition. What do I have left to prove, and to whom.

Good morning.

Barbara Jane Reyes
26 mins · 🌐 ▾

This is how women, WOC, APIA women, Pinay writers and artists get erased
though. You work your heart and soul into your art, fight like hell to be
recognized, sometimes by establishment, sometimes by your own community,
who will overlook you constantly because you're not the right kind of anything.
You are the only one pushing your work. You exhaust yourself. You need to
tend to your life, and there are so many other women pressured into leaving
professional lives because it is still unconventional for a woman to have a
public life, rather than do the private, the uncompensated domestic,
reproductive labor.

When you "leave" the industry, everyone forgets you, erases you, because you
are not there to advocate for yourself. Also, you've gotten old anyway, and the
world you live in really doesn't like older women so much. Decades pass. Your
work is out of print. Maybe in the next century, that work will be "recovered,"
"uncovered," "discovered." Or maybe it won't.

So this is the answer to my own question, about why I am not so chill.

This is where I am this morning, threatening to leave the industry again, and thinking about why I stick it out. There's a name I've been hearing about — Felicidad V. Ocampo. Two novels of hers were published in this country, and they both predate Carlos Bulosan. But you won't hear much about her.

I've been teaching the (short form) writings of Yay Panlilio Marking and Helen Rillera in my Pinay Lit class at USF. If not for scholar Denise Cruz, I would have never heard of Marking. If not for scholar and artist Jean Vengua, I would have never heard of Rillera. And there at Vengua's Commonwealth Cafe website, she discussed the work of recovery, and her wide casting of nets to find Pinays' writings, into the Op Eds in Filipino American community newspapers and newsletters. I also teach Angeles Monrayo's diary, *Tomorrow's Memories*, and Dawn Bohulano Mabalon's Afterword to the volume, so we can rethink "Pinay absence," in Filipino American History. My students talk about Monrayo, and why she stopped writing in her diary. This coincides with her becoming a wife and a mother. As with Rillera, we talk about these "non-literary" genres, and is this why these women are so obscured. But Ocampo had two novels published. Novels are revered in American Letters. And yet, we know little about her work. We can't find her work.

When I teach Marking, Rillera, and Monrayo, I talk about recoveries of buried work, and we talk a bit about why their writings have been buried in the first place. But what I do not stress enough is that our community is so invested in championing the works of some, eclipsing all others.

Today, when conceivably everyone is "findable," people ask me all the time, "What ever happened to Catalina Cariaga? She has dropped off the map." Some people ask me whether Virginia Cerenio and Shirley Ancheta ever published again, and what ever happened to them. And perhaps the answer is that we can make ourselves "unfindable" if we don't want to be found, but more so, that if we are not aggressively sticking our necks out there on the regular, we disappear from public view.

The truth is, I am exhausted. But the truth also is that I fear erasure. I resent the possibility of erasure. I resent the institutional reasons why I, why someone like me, may be erased.

May 24, 2018 #APAHM #APIAHeritageMonth: Time for Some Author Introspection

APIA Heritage Month is drawing to a close. I don't know that I accomplished much out there, in the big world, apart from surviving my last semester of teaching an enormous Filipino Lit class. I did a cluster of book events, readings, which were difficult for me; my voice cracking and my being breathless throughout, and so I have been thinking about this difficulty.

Invocation to Daughters is a hard book. I have so much in it I am so emotionally close to. There are also bluntly stated brutalities in it that are hard to read aloud to audiences, and to discuss with students. These brutalities are contained in what I worked really hard to make poetically sound, and even manageable. Yes, this is the power of poetry, to make appear manageable what is not ... and should not be?

To Love as Aswang was also filled with brutalities, but the reach of this book was considerably "smaller" than *Invocation to Daughters,* and so discussion felt contained. It has also appealed to a different kind of reader of poetry, someone who never considered themselves a reader or subject of literary works.

I don't know that I had this kind of emotional difficulty with *Poeta en San Francisco,* speaking of farther reach. I was so young in poetry, which made me brave. I had a lot of energy to be "out there," defending my shit and arguing hard online on my own behalf. I had a lot of confidence in rallying "allies" against (white, male) internet bullies. I thought fracas made my work cool, that it was a measure of its success.

I see when other writers and authors shrink from public view. Being in the public view is not safe. It's almost counterintuitive, to put all your deepest shit on blast, and appear perfectly comfortable discussing this with total strangers. For me, that's all performance. You're on a stage, enacting a public persona. There may be pieces of that public persona that approximate your true self (whatever that is), but it sure gets difficult over time to be in that performative space.

For WOC, for Filipina Americans in public, literary spaces, it takes a toll, all of this white supremacist and patriarchal crap to which we are called upon to respond — another day, another white male writer/ public figure saying something racist and misogynistic, that everyone has made their business on social media. How to make people care about work in my community, when we know that in life outside literature, they will never give a fuck about people like us, and what we have to say when we speak on our own behalf.

For a while I felt like I could open my personal me to the poetry, which the readers I was trying to reach seem to respond well to. I am now here, after I read, "The Day," having had strangers in public spaces open up to me to tell me about their grieving, which is beautiful and difficult to do in crowded rooms of people I don't know. I have also had strangers tell me to my face that I could have done more to keep my father alive. What I do not say is, Who the fuck are you, telling me this to my face, like you know me and my family. Fuck you and your armchair judgment. And this too, is the beauty and difficulty of poetry.

Perhaps these are ways of telling that the poetry is effective, that people actually listen and process, and perhaps you will tell me I must weigh the "good" and the "bad" that come with my chosen path, that it evens out in the end, that it is a good problem to have, people in public talking about your work, talking to you about your work, responding to your work because they took the time to listen to you and form an opinion and feel something. I am inclined to agree, and I also know it's wearing me down.

I have been asking myself whether I should want to continue sharing these deepest, most honest things in my work, and it is making me unsure of where I want my next manuscript to go when it finally leaves my hard drive. What will it, and I go through, once it's in the world. I see why other writers go the route of crafting clever and quirky public personae as a kind of social protection. I see it, I get it, and I also hate it, seeing POC writers having to make themselves socially neuter as a strategy, or falsely transcendent, or falsely disaffected, looking obviously disingenuous. I think this too, is the opposite of bravery. I can't help but think, might this also stunt the growth of the artist and the art.

I don't have a tidy resolution here. I'm just in this space, and I don't know yet what to do with it. I know readers in my community who want honesty and social relevance, not cleverness and artifice, and I love that about them. I want to keep bringing it, and I don't want it to break me.

September 19, 2018 The Making of a Book: Letters to a Young Brown Girl

I want to be as real as I can, about how painstaking, tedious, exhausting, self-reflective, joy- and wonder-filled, and rewarding this whole process of writing, editing, revising a book to a polish, seeing it find a great home, and seeing it connect with community is.

My forthcoming book, *Letters to a Young Brown Girl*, consists of three parts: (1) Brown Girl Desig(n)ation, (2) Brown Girl Mixtape, and (3) Letters to a Young Brown Girl.

I started writing poems for this collection in a couple of different places. First, I was collecting language about "beauty," as defined by the beauty industry. What were all of my Sephora and Ulta emails telling me I needed to consume, to part with my hard earned cash, in order to achieve or attain beauty. We consume beauty, and we consent to its narrow definitions. When we do not fit these narrow definitions of beauty, what happens to us. How do others view us. How do others treat us. How do we view ourselves. What do we do to ourselves. This is gendered. This is class-based. This is age-based. This is racial, and cultural.

This consumable beauty, as per the beauty industry, has larger implications. What is our value, as women, as women of color, as immigrants, as citizens. Do we let others determine that value for us. What others. Why do we give them power over us. Do we have a choice. What happens when we try to wrest that power back. What happens when we can't even recognize how crippled by, and how inculcated we are into that larger structure, such that we have lost our ability (and/or will) to envision. Or, what are the consequences of trying to envision a different kind of structure. Who's policing us but our own. Why.

This is the context in which I started writing my letters to many young — and not so young — brown girls. I put out a call to fellow Filipinas. I asked them, what do you need to ask me. There were so many questions about writing as an "ethnic," "foreign" person in the literary publishing industry. So much anxiety, so much fear of our own "foreignness." So much fear of standing out as "alien." So much fear of white and male reprisal. I return to my Sephora and Ulta inspired poems. We fear not fitting into that narrow standard of beauty. We fear rejection. We relate rejection with self-worth. All of this fear of institutional rejection becomes the major determining factor for whether we even speak at all. It doesn't occur to us that there are alternative structures where we do belong. It doesn't occur to us that those alternative structures are not of lesser value.

When I first started writing these poems, the working title of my manuscript was "some brown girl." It didn't know its purpose. It wasn't getting to what I wanted this work to do. Retitling it *Letters to a Young*

Brown Girl gave me direction. It put human relationship and human connection on the line. It made care rise to prominence.

The epistolary is intimate and personalized. It is earnest and honest. It is emotional. And it is highly curated. Before email, before texting, epistolary was a manual and tactile art making. It was handwritten with just the right writing implement — ink color, nib or point, heft of the thing in your hand — on just the right paper — wide, college, or narrow ruled, grid, weight and texture, color, stationery design — with the right postage stamps — hearts, rainbows, comic book characters, historical figures. All of this speaks to meaningful, high emotional stakes human connection. It also speaks of aesthetics.

I return to my study, growing understanding, and practice of Filipino core values and concepts, which for me become the heart of the matter — kapwa, loób. In other words, I return to my center. I write from there. I write with the most confidence when I write from there. And I write with the most confidence because I remember why it is I love to write, and why I chose poetry. Before I ever became an adult. Before I went to college. Before I considered the MFA route. Before I knew anything about this industry. I wrote because writing was my process for understanding my own belief system, for understanding where I come from and where I'm at, for understanding who "my people" are, those with whom I wish or aspire to make meaningful connection. Writing poetry is my way of understanding this world, and my way of reaching outside of myself.

A more accessible means of communication for those like me, thwarted by "High Literature," is the mixtape, where tone/mood, rhythm/music, and lyric intersect in accessible units and media. You think about transition and arc, individual song message and tone, and larger body message being conveyed. Before digital music, constructing mixtape was a manual and tactile labor of love. It was DIY. It was gift and keepsake.

Aren't these the places we come to understand how we are connected to one another, how we come to see ourselves in one another – kapwa. Aren't these the places where soul-baring necessarily happens – loób.

Is it naive for me to want to return to that personalized, curated labor of love, especially living within all encompassing capitalism, where everything is up for consumption. Where all human relationships are reduced to consumer relationships. I don't want to accept this as naïveté. So this is *Letters to a Young Brown Girl*. I promise it's full of (tough) love.

October 29, 2018 About "Filipinos Do Not Read"

Fellow Pinay authors and educators Gayle Romasanta and Dawn Bohulano Mabalon (RIP) have focused some much needed attention on younger readers in our community. At Bridge and Delta Publishing, their *Journey for Justice: The Life of Larry Itliong* just launched this past weekend in San Francisco. I see there was a packed house, generations of folks and families. I am heartened by this enthusiasm.

Allyson Tintiangco-Cubales created Pin@y Educational Partnerships (PEP) back in 2001, in order to intervene in curricula, with the assertion that our invisibility in American curricula and our community's social problems are not mutually exclusive.

At the beginning of each semester, I always ask my students for a show of hands: Who here has ever read a book authored by a Filipino? Who here has ever read a book authored by a Filipino American? Who here has ever read a book authored by a Pinay?

Usually, zero or one hand goes up.

I tell them, in 15 weeks, you will have read so many more Filipino authored books than many people in our community will in their lifetime. I tell them, I can only hope you will continue on, after you leave this classroom, and into the world. In addition to my courses' required texts, I provide recommended reading lists in multiple genres — full volumes, anthologies/collections, as well as links to individual pieces published online.

Some may never read another Filipino authored book; they got a pretty good grade, and they got course credit, and it fulfilled the literature and diversity requirements, and that's what they came for — I am glad they did it with Filipino Literature. I can't complain. College is expensive; our culture does not encourage "curiosity," "exploration," and "discovery" as much as getting equipped for the working world. But I am happy to say, they will walk into the world armed with knowledge, and maybe even wisdom, and self-reflection.

Sometimes, I feel that by the time a 20-year old is reading their first Filipino authored book for my class, it's almost too late. The void has been so normalized, as if we were never told that Filipino authored books existed in this country, and as if we believed them and internalized that void.

Some Filipino American students will straight up say, where has this book been all of my life. I wish I had read this when I was young. This is the case with *The Land of Forgotten Girls*, by Erin Entrada Kelly. Erin is a prolific author of middle grade novels, which means young people are reading stories about young Filipino Americans. Imagine, if we'd had books like this, from a young Filipina American's perspective, when we were very young. What would the emotional impact be of having this book, alongside M. Evelina Galang's *One Tribe*, these narratives of young Pinays living, struggling, and learning.

In the big publishing industry: Erin also recently won the Newbery Award. This means more and more young people in this country are and will be reading stories about young Filipino Americans. And at my most optimistic, I think and hope this leads to the publication of more young Filipino American texts. Publishing in this country moves slowly in the right direction. Elaine Castillo's *America is Not the Heart* has been critically acclaimed and wide-reaching. And Trinidad Escobar's *Of Sea and Venom* and Melissa Chadburn's *A Tiny Upward Shove* were recently picked up by Farrar, Straus and Giroux. All of these things mean something to Filipinos in this country who have never seen themselves in books.

How do we get those interested in the "big" works also interested the independent and small press offerings, as opposed to believing only a small handful writers exist, that there are no others. Surely, these big transactions get books onto people's radars. Big contracts, big publishing houses, big awards – when Jessica Hagedorn's *Dogeaters* finalisted for the National Book Award, not to mention when it was reviewed for big venues such as the *New York Times* and *Vogue*, a lot of people picked up the book. They read it, and even if they hated it (look at the Amazon reviews), they took the time to read it, to think about it, to feel something about it, and to share their feelings in public forums.

In my classrooms, my students aren't so outraged by *Dogeaters*. Surely this has to do with the disconnect, as the book is 27 years old, and written about another time and place for my mostly young, mostly American students, many of whom are the children and grandchildren of Filipino immigrants. But it's also because narrative strategies branded as "postmodern" have become much utilized in today's popular storytelling.

And in my classrooms, some students do share with their families and friends what they are reading – a student recently told me she told her father about Angeles Monrayo's *Tomorrow's Memories*, because this was her family's history too, as descendants of Filipino agricultural laborers in Hawaii. Monrayo's diaries, chronicling her everyday life of labor and hustle, resonate. This is no exaggeration then, when I say that students see themselves in these works.

Students' word of mouth brings more students into my classrooms, and to my events. In other words, the work has moved them; they found something in it they needed, enjoyed, or made them really think. My classes fill so fast; my class sizes have grown, and I love all of this enthusiasm in Filipino authored texts, overwhelmed as I am with class size. How can I bring all of this "important" work to them, from publishers big and small, from authors global and local.

This is a great problem to have. I share these here, because it's important that all of us know how enthusiastic young people are for our literature. That there is interest, even in the works conventionally defined as "difficult," whether it's difficulty in content and subject matter, such as *To Love as Aswang* and *Invocation to Daughters*, and Elynia S. Mabanglo's *Anyaya ng Imperyalista*, or difficulty in form, construction, or experiment, such as Cheena Marie Lo's *A Series of Un/Natural/Disasters*, or Wilfrido D. Nolledo's *But for the Lovers*. Nolledo's dense and lyrical "experimental" narrative strategies haven't become as accessible as *Dogeaters* potentially is now.

All of this to say,

1. I support and applaud the work of those making Filipino American authored texts accessible to young readers. A Filipino American bookseller told me many years ago that books for young people were a harder sell because you had to rely on the parents to bring these books to their children. That was a different time, because now, it seems some sectors of Filipino American parents are indeed voicing that hunger for books for young readers. Sometimes, it's for themselves, because they'd never had the opportunity, and want to start somewhere (they're experiencing the "where were these books when I was young").

2. I support and applaud those educators bringing Filipino authored texts into their curricula, whether it's classes in Filipino Lit, Asian American Lit, American Lit, American Poetry, and so on.

3. I support and applaud the Filipino authors hustling to get their best works into the world. There are the big names, the big publishers, the big transactions. There are the small press authors and publishers. Our community's authors are in many places, and really comprise many different communities. The hunger to get our work out there is real, and I would like to gently remind folks — no pressure — this is much larger and more important than our own egos and individual careers. Every publication can be an opportunity to connect with a Filipino reader.

4. I am forever grateful for the supporters, the editors — Eileen Tabios, Cecilia Manguerra Brainard, Nick Carbó, Luisa Igloria, Edwin Lozada. The curators — PJ Gubatina Policarpio. The librarians — Estela Manila, Mitchell Yangson, Abraham Ignacio. The booksellers — Eastwind Books of Berkeley, Arkipelago Books. The book reviewers, the buyers of books, the gifters of books. Too many people to name. Even someone who does not think they have "cultural capital," can support. Support comes in many forms, so thank you.

January 10, 2019 Writing post patriarchy in 2019

Hello everyone,

Will we ever get to writing and living post-patriarchy. I mean, you can do all this "clean up," in your own personal life, and walk out the front door, and immediately have patriarchy inflicted upon you.

Anyway, I'm writing about this today, as part of an explanation for what I'd like to come after *Letters to a Young Brown Girl*, whether it's possible to ever be post-patriarchy when the writer is writing, fully entrenched in critically examining those value systems.

If we have chosen hetero marriages, I wonder what is our relationship to the traditional institution of marriage — are we changing anything if we've examined and shifted towards equal sharing of "power," or by virtue of our participation in the institution, are we still perpetuating its traditional values. I wonder this, after having been subjected for years to people — from relatives to total fucking strangers — chastising me one way or another for not having children. When I'd put on a few pounds, relatives would ask me if I was pregnant. I've had folks overwhelmed to death with their kids, struggling paycheck to paycheck, bags under their eyes, defeat in their body language, still rabidly shouting at me, "OH MY GOD BARB, YOU TOTALLY HAVE TO HAVE KIDS!"; when I was single, in grad school, financially unstable, and not seeing anyone of reliable reputation, I had people telling me I should totally do it, just be a single mom. Why would anybody wish this baggage upon me? I guess they were worried that I was single, in my mid-30s, biological clock, yadda yadda. I guess they were worried about my life choices. I guess they were really, more deeply worried that my life choices could have also been their choices, if they had chosen differently, they too could have gone to art school, prioritized learning and creativity, had their time be their own. Worlds are turned upside down because some of us choose not to be defined as wives and mothers. Articulating any kind of rejection of these values always makes a conversation awkward.

So in *Letters to a Young Brown Girl*, I do write about how, no matter what choices we make, we will always be chastised for having not made the right choice. There is never a right choice, in the eyes of folks fully invested in perpetuating patriarchal values. We're supposed to just accept people's impositions into our personal lives. We're supposed to accept people speaking of our bodies as hyper-public common property, cattle, specimens to prod and magnify and display.

Now, I am seeing major media news outlets' articles voicing the concern that "millennials" are not having babies, and so America is in trouble. And I'm like, don't we have a population and resource crisis. We don't house and care for our own citizens, and how do you want to coerce people into having babies, for moms who may be saddled in debt, who may not have health insurance, who may not have job and housing security, so that the next generation can also struggle to get an education and not have health insurance, and so on. (End rant.)

I say all this now, to talk about the "crisis" being one of patriarchal concern. Is our culture shifting, such that traditional roles defined by patriarchal standards are eroding. I ask this as an optimist. Is this us inching towards post-patriarchy. Speculative poetry must now happen, to imagine or envision that post-patriarchal society. This is where I want my poetry to go. What is this poetry going to look like. What would my poetry look like, if I were to write as if there were never patriarchy, as if it's not even in my mind. No bitches, no monsters, no creative survival mechanisms. Just interior lives of those living in non-patriarchy. Or is this uncompelling. Is it our struggle in the real world we appreciate reading about, precisely because we take these to heart for ways to conduct ourselves and cope in the real world.

January 11, 2019 In 2019: post-patriarchy, cont., or, are there men of color who owe you an apology

Are there men of color who owe you an apology, and if so, what do we do about it.

I've been sitting on a lot of emotions about this, cutting toxic masculinity out of my social circles — men who dismiss me, feel entitled to my time, men who repackage and take credit for the things I say. I also internalize a lot, as do many of us. I go through these periods of thinking, "well, maybe I spoke out of turn," "maybe I should have minded my tone." Then I get back to my senses. I want to ask, why aren't they expected to apologize to us for oppressing their own community members. Why aren't they held accountable. Why do our communities uphold and enable them. Why do our communities celebrate them.

When we speak, pay attention to who shuts us down, belittles us, throws blame back at us, straight up act like we didn't speak at all. Pay attention to how frequently this happens.

Speaking in public for WOC, for Pinays is always going to be thought of as speaking out of turn. Writing in public as WOC, as Pinays, is always going to be thought of as speaking out of turn. Doing these things without permission, speaking and writing without pre-approval of our content, brings consequence.

The softness of tone and subject matter that is demanded of us is gendered, and it is another way of saying to us, do not say anything controversial or confrontational. Do not say anything of consequence. Do not say anything.

How do we change this.

I am always interested in how we always want to place this back on whiteness. I agree that it's white supremacy and patriarchy at work when we're shut down for speaking our minds, putting "unapproved" messages out there. But I want to think about who enforces white supremacy and patriarchy among our ranks. Who benefits from our being shut down. How can we call this out without being shut down further.

Or are we OK with perpetually being branded bitches — or crazy bitches, thereby being socially shunned. Is there another way. Where are the places our bravery is truly valued. You may say, here, and now, we value your bravery. But I want you also to think about how you are afraid of it, how you wish we would just not speak because you are afraid of the consequences brought to you for being associated with our so-called bravery. Whether you're actually more comfortable viewing this all at a safe distance, whether you'd prefer not to view it at all.

Is there another way, that does not entail internalizing the very value systems which oppress and negate us. I want to hear it. Or are we always going to have to be the crazy bitches unless we just shut up and accept our silence.

January 12, 2019 In 2019: post-patriarchy, cont., again and again, post-patriarchy

To have your goals and ambitions laid out before you, the goals and ambitions of somebody else, fully vetted to be non-controversial, for social acceptability, to be inconsequential. To be cast as a barren old maid. To be cast as the difficult one. To be told, you will never marry a doctor with that attitude and itsura. To be told to have light skinned children. To have men talk over you constantly. To have them raise their voices to drown you out. They won't let you finish. To be told, you shouldn't speak in the first place. To have women back away from you, no one come to your defense. To have women also chastise you, for being too much this, not enough that. To be told you have brought all of this upon yourself. You are alone and this is of your own making. To be told, you should have just married well, become a mother. To be told, you have to make nice. To be told, don't make waves.

When I was young, I was rebellious. I didn't know yet, exactly the heart of what I was rebelling against. I was rebellious because I wanted to be cool. Like James Dean, *Rebel Without a Cause* cool. I didn't know any rebellious girls, and so my role models were rebellious boys, rockstars. The alternative was to want to be a video girl, a flirty, sexy, skimpy dressed girl in high heels and make-up. That was also appealing, but more appealing was The Rockstar. The Lyricist. The Front (Wo)man.

The Romantic Poet, a someone who could speak and write the words no one else around me was saying (yet).

This is one impetus behind my "Brown Girl Mixtape" in *Letters to a Young Brown Girl*, a constellation of brown and Black women, women of color front and center, lyricizing.

February 16, 2019 Sometimes, many times, wanting to become a writer is like this.

Barbara Jane Reyes
February 14 at 9:13 AM · 🌐 ▾

The first time I collected my poems into what could have been a cohesive body of work, was in a private, blue marbled, hardcover journal with gold leafed book page edges, handwritten in pink or purple ink, with a Waterman fountain pen.

The second time I collected my poems into what could have been a cohesive body of work, was in a private, purple, three-ring binder, with poems printed in papyrus font, each page in its own plastic page protector.

We start in all kinds of small places, with romantic ideas of what poetry should be, and how it should look. This is a necessary exercise in envisioning possibility.

Barbara Jane Reyes
February 14 at 10:26 AM · 🌐 ▾

The third time I collected my poems into what could have been a cohesive body of work, was in a class portfolio in a Berkeley City College poetry class I took after I graduated from UC Berkeley. It consisted of ten poems I wrote during the semester, experimenting with white space; this became the portfolio of poems I submitted to the one MFA program I applied to. Many of these poems made it into the first section of my first book, Gravities of Center.

The fourth time I collected my poems into what could have been a cohesive body of work, was in a DIY chapbook I made on my work PC, copied, collated, and stapled at Fed Ex Kinkos in Downtown Oakland, sold out of my backpack, and at the zine fest of Kearny Street Workshop's APAture.

Barbara Jane Reyes
Yesterday at 8:47 AM · 🌐 ▾

The fifth time I collected my poems into what could have been a cohesive body of work, these were the poems from Berkeley City College, my MFA application portfolio, my DIY chapbook, and with editorial work from Eileen Tabios, this became my first book, Gravities of Center.

This is a frequently forgotten book, one barely taken seriously if thought about at all, locally produced and distributed, entirely outside of the much revered enormous monster we call Po Biz, by an SF based Pinay entrepreneur.

The sixth time I collected my poems into a cohesive body of work was my MFA thesis, Poeta en San Francisco. With very minimal changes, it was accepted for publication by Tinfish Press, one of maybe five publishers I submitted it to. This was my second book. It won the James Laughlin Award.

Next year, my sixth book goes into production. All this to say, it takes many tries, many times. And if we're serious about writing and publishing, we don't belittle any of this work of arrival.

This is what I've been posting about on social media, this work of arriving, and especially the first steps, private, painfully self-conscious, at times pretentious, but so important for momentum. When I was in college, especially when I was indefinitely dropped out of college, I did a lot of floundering because I didn't know what I wanted to do with myself. I thought I wanted to write, but I didn't know what to do in order to become a writer. So I was stuck, and part of it was feeling so stunted from not being able to finish college. I eventually did, of course, after I just couldn't stand it anymore, being so sad all the time, wanting so bad to do something, but not doing it, and not knowing why you're not doing it. And then making excuses for not doing it.

Sometimes, many times, wanting to become a writer is like this. I think we all know — we'd have to be in utter denial not to — that becoming a writer is work. Studying, reading, thinking — all of these are work. And writing is work. Even if we love it, it's work. I say these things, because no matter what people say, we value writing because it's work, because it's hard work.

I remember my private journals full of proto-poetry, inchoate poems, overwrought and earnest, writings entirely unpublishable, evidence that I was beginning to envision and practice committing my words to the page, editing, tweaking word choices, line breaks that weren't quite there, weren't quite right. I was experimenting. My journals were hardcover, marbled, glossy. The pages were edged in gold leaf. The pens I used to hand write my poems in these marbled journals were fountain pens — at first, Pilot Varsity disposable fountain pens. And then a Waterman Laureat fountain pen, also blue marbled. Super fancy. I was creating, building a kind of poet-ness about me. I was all about English Romantic poetry, but without formal knowledge of romanticism and rebellion (I might have had an inkling; it had to appeal to me for some reason).

All of this before I ever finished college, before I ever took creative writing classes. Everything I had written up to this point was all instinctive. Lots of copying the styles of others (see "English Romantic poetry," above), work you would call derivative. I say all of this, because it's important to start somewhere. Envision the thing, get yourself into place, start figuring out how to plan, start trying to do the thing. Learn to be brave. This can happen slowly, and that's fine. This isn't a race.

Certainly, it helped to find mentors who expressed interest in what work I had already done; it helped tremendously that they gave me some of their space and time. I wish I could tell you what they saw in me. Earnestness? Hunger? Persistence? (Heaven forbid,) talent? These were the folks who propelled me into my graduate program, into publishing, and further into publishing. After *Poeta en San Francisco*, one of my mentors immediately checked in with me to say, this is great, but what are you working on now; keep moving. I then asked another one of my mentors his opinion about one of the small presses I'd thought of submitting my *Diwata* manuscript to. He told me I could do better by my work. He told me to be more ambitious, think bigger, aim higher.

I write all of this, hoping I am being helpful. Young people do ask all the time, how I came to do what I do. They wonder how they may also. I share what I can. I do my best to be both encouraging and real. Anything worth pursuing is going to be hard work. Be wary of those offering you shortcuts, cut corners, glossing over the details of what the work entails. Be realistic with your expectations. Be prepared to work hard. Expect critique. Expect to be humbled. Take nothing for granted.

December 16, 2019 We get into poetry the way we get into poetry

There's a story that Jason Bayani tells often; I read it in his author interviews. In the mid-1990s, he attended a spoken word event in a community center in Oakland. There, he saw me perform. And this is where it was clarified for him that that's what he wanted to do, perform spoken word.

That event was organized and curated by Pinoy DJ Klay Ordoña, now known as DJ Bruddah K, aka Kayumanggi. The event was a July 4th event, featuring POC/BIPOC artists — I didn't have the critical language for it then, but we were engaging in a kind of anti-colonial performance.

I remember each of us performed either music, or spoken word. I remember the piece I performed was about a photograph of a young Filipina holding a semi-automatic weapon. I knew nothing about her, but a friend had given me that photograph, and told me that she was me. I remember a young Native American poet whose piece was about coming up in subsidized housing in the city. I remember singing and drumming. I remember that at the end of the individual performances, everyone — performers and audience together — standing in a circle participating in an improvised song. I remember everyone in the room in or near tears.

The venue was Rafiq Bilal's Nu Upper Room in Oakland, where folks like KRS One and The Last Poets had performed. I didn't know then, what any of that meant. I was in my mid-20s. I didn't know what I was doing with my life, but I did know that when I was onstage, I was brave. I had never taken creative writing before. I wrote from gut and heart. I had this vague idea that "spoken word" was something I was good at, though I'm not so sure I could have told you why. I wrote and performed like crazy. And then in 1999, the well ran dry, and I wrote exactly one poem. I finished my degree that year. I was 28.

I write this now, to think about how I knew — or didn't know — that I would ever be a poet. Folks ask me now, who was I reading back then, who was I studying with, and didn't I know there were American poets of renown in my midst.

The answer to the second and third questions are that I wasn't and didn't. I didn't know the American poets of renown around me. All I knew was that I was reading Kearny Street Workshop folks and POC — I had been an opening poet for Jaime Jacinto's book launch for *Heaven is Just Another Country*. I read Ntozake Shange's *for colored girls who have considered suicide when the rainbow is enuf*. I read Jessica Hagedorn's *Dangerous Music*. I knew Maxine Hong Kingston taught at UC Berkeley, though I was never able to take her classes; I was too busy trying to cram all my major requirements into a tight schedule while I worked full time, as clerical staff for private practice physicians. This is where I met Czeslaw Milosz, not as a poet, but as a client of the practice. This is also where I met Nanos Valaoritis, a City Lights poet, in the same capacity.

I was stagnant; all attempts at writers' groups were falling through. After my 1990s spoken word rush, filled with joyful brown folks creating and exuberant sharing, I had no idea what to do next. After I finally graduated from college, I finally took a creative writing class in 2000, a poetry class at Berkeley City College, and I was broken wide open. The following semester, in 2001, I was in an MFA program. In 2003, my first book was published locally, by a Pinay owned press no one in the "right" places in poetry care about. That first book brought me to places I didn't even know I was ever capable of going.

We get into poetry the way we get into poetry. There is no right or wrong way. I'm done with those who shame folks for not reading the "right" poets, and for liking Instagram poetry or song lyrics, for the prestige-less small and micro presses that publish their work. Folks are hella mean to one another for not getting and having the "right" things, and so it's no wonder emotions run high in this field. I have since learned that in fact, you can still have all the "right" things, degrees, book contracts with the "right" publishers, awards from the "right" awarding bodies, and still be chastised for not writing the "right" way. If I have any kind of wisdom to impart — for aspiring and emerging poets, read what you like (do read!), write what and how you like. Put your work out there. Just do the damn thing.

December 26, 2019 In the Filipino Diaspora, We Are Remaking Tradition, the Recipe Edition

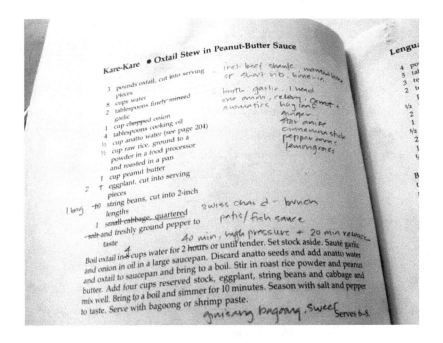

This is my copy of Reynaldo Alejandro, *The Philippine Cookbook* (NY: Perigee Books, 1985).

As you can see, I have made some amendments to my oldest Filipino cookbook, which I have had since the 1990s.

No one ever really taught me to cook. I've been making kare kare for a few years now, for Christmas dinner with my mother's side of the family. I now make kare kare at least once a year. Prior to this, I was in charge of the pochero, which also no one ever taught me how to cook. So I write this, not as a chef, but as a daughter.

I started with this cookbook, Reynaldo Alejandro's *The Philippine Cookbook*, which, as you can see, is well worn. Each time I cook, I tweak some things. I was told I should write this down one day. I think of my fellow Pinay authors, who, when asking their elder women how you "know" family recipe measurements, you usually get a "just add some.." "just some..." "just a little of..." and I see how this can be maddening. But for myself, I think I get it. We pick up these family traditions not through any formal education or rite of passage, but simply by having it in our lives, in our family homes, in our family celebrations. We may ask an elder woman, with our modern ideas of recipe, but the elder women just did it, and continued to do it for years, for their whole lives.

By the time I was old enough to try to make any of these dishes, my mother's mother had long passed. My mom and her sisters would tell me what they knew, and their knowledge came from having these things in their lives, in their homes for as long as they could remember. When I told my mom I didn't really like cabbage or bok choy in kare kare, she said, just switch it out. She recommended Swiss chard, and so now, I use rainbow chard because it's aesthetically pleasing. When I told her I couldn't find oxtails because I'd gone to the butcher too late in the Christmas season, she said, try shank or short rib. I started adding these aromatics to the broth because they were in my spice cabinet. A cinnamon stick, some star anise. This time around, since we were at the Whole Foods produce section, I said, let's use lemongrass too.

I am writing this for those of you asking. And so I'm telling you to do it your way. I'm telling you to ask your family what, why, and how. Why does your family do things the way they do. How did their/your traditions change over time, with migration and economics. I am writing this, because I want to say a few things about tradition. In my family, it's generally women's tradition.

As I've been teaching Pinay Lit for almost a decade now, one thing we talk about is where women create and convey narrative, when they do not have access to literacy, and/or to formal education. In my family, many of my elder women did go to school. And though they did have lives in the working world, they were also the keepers of family tradition. Many things did change, not from negligence or even rebellion, but just from economics, and availability of food items and time. In recent years, my mother and her sisters have given a lot of this responsibility to me and my sisters.

I have no family recipe book; I was recently watching Jacques Pépin on PBS, and he showed his books of meals — what was served for what courses on what dates, and who was at the dinner party. These are artful heirlooms. These are the things that matter. I recently read Betty

Ann Quirino's "Last Christmas," where she writes about what you take with you, what you hold close, what changes, and what matters.

I think a lot of people misunderstand these days and just want the cheap and easy answer that would best be answered through introspection and talking to their own families. A friend of mine just posted his photos of his homemade ensaymadas, and then he wrote, these are from my lola's recipe, which he didn't share. He shared a recipe that was already posted online. For him, his lola's recipe is sacred. Others would demand he share, say he's being selfish, hoarding knowledge. No, he's holding his lola's memory close, precisely because it is sacred. Sometimes, these are the only things we have left of our elder women.

For me, it's deep. I think of my mother and her sisters handing this responsibility over to me. On the surface, you see me raving about my Instant Pot, but I'm thinking of my mother's mother. I'm thinking, how can I have inherited so much from her, when I still have a million questions I will never be able to ask her.

February 12, 2020 What are 20 poetry books that made you fall in love with poetry

A few years ago, February 22, 2009 to be exact, I was asked this question via blog meme:

What are 20 poetry books (if there are twenty) that made you fall in love with poetry, the books that made you think: I want to do this, I need to do this. What are the books that kept you going? Don't put down the books that you think you're "supposed" to like, but list the core ones, the ones that opened all of this up for you.

On February 22, 2009, this was my list of 20:

1. Ntozake Shange, *For Colored Girls Who Have Considered Suicide When the Rainbow Is Enuf.*
2. Jessica Hagedorn, *Dangerous Music.*
3. Myung Mi Kim, *Under Flag.*
4. Bhanu Kapil, *The Vertical Interrogation of Strangers.*
5. Catalina Cariaga, *Cultural Evidence.*
6. Federico García Lorca, *Poeta en Nueva York.*
7. Jimmy Santiago Baca, *Martín & Meditations on the South Valley.*
8. Truong Tran, *Dust and Conscience.*
9. Jaime Jacinto, *Heaven is Just Another Country.*
10. Frances Chung, *Crazy Melon and Chinese Apple.*
11. Harryette Mullen, *Recyclopedia.*
12. Gloria Anzaldúa, *Borderlands/La Frontera.*
13. Leslie Marmon Silko, *Storyteller.*
14. Anne Waldman, *Fast Speaking Woman.*
15. Theresa Hak Kyung Cha, *Dictee.*
16. Oliver de la Paz, *Names Above Houses.*
17. Allen Ginsberg, *Howl.*
18. Bay Area Pilipino American Writers (eds.), *Without Names.*
19. Merlinda Bobis, *Cantata of the Woman Warrior Daragang Magayon.*
20. Walter Lew (ed.), *Premonitions.*

I also included these additional thoughts:

- R. Zamora Linmark's *Rolling the R's* is a novel, which consists of vignettes and many poems, and which has strongly informed my code switching and use of Catholic prayer.
- Eduardo Galeano is not considered a poet, though his numerous volumes of genre blurring work is to me very much poetry. Also, his reading and interview in the Lannan video series made me simply giddy.
- Mahmoud Darwish's *Memory For Forgetfulness* is an extended meditation on exile, which to me reads as one very long prose poem.
- Trinh Minh-ha's *Woman, Native, Other* is not poetry, although her discussions of women of color artists, and post-colonialism have been very important to my poetics.
- Lawrence Ferlinghetti's *Poetry as Insurgent Art* is really quite lovely. I realize this sounds demeaning, but I mean this sincerely. There are so many bits of taken for granted common sense and illumination in this collection, stuff I need badly to remember when careless people and the Poetic Industrial Complex drag me down.

That was 2009. At that time, I was admonished by someone (two guesses what gender and ethnicity said giver of admonition was), that my list was too provincial, too contemporary, lacking in the great enduring classics and canonical works. Obviously, this person had his own ideas and context with little intersection to or consideration of my own context.

I know I had answered as honestly as possible; I always say — and it's the absolute truth — that if I had never seen, encountered poetry collections from fierce, indie WOC and POC, especially Filipino Americans, especially Filipino Americans in the Bay Area, then the likelihood of my pursuing a career in letters would have been near impossible.

What saddens me most and what grosses me out is that we still don't allow or give space for people to find their own ways into poetry, whatever route, whatever timetable. And we just don't let folks love the poetry they love.

I wanted to revisit this list, especially this part of the question: works "that made you fall in love with poetry, the books that made you think: I want to do this, I need to do this." I wanted to think about how I, a decade later, would amend my 2009 list above. And maybe the way to word it now would be like this: stripped of all the noise and hype, what books make you rethink, make you challenge and reevaluate your own poetics, rekindle your love for, your faith in poetry, and in what poetry can do. That said, my list grows, and will continue to grow:

1. Al Robles, *rapping with ten thousand carabaos in the dark*.
2. Nick Carbó, *El Grupo McDonald's*.
3. Yoko Ono, *Grapefruit*.
4. Ambar Past, Xalik Guzmán Bakbolom, Xpetra Ernandes, *Incantation: Songs, Spells and Images by Mayan Women*.
5. Mila D. Aguilar, *A Comrade is as Precious as a Rice Seedling*.
6. Elynia S. Mabanglo, *Anyaya ng Imperyalista: Mga Tula / Invitation of the Imperialist*.
7. Joy Harjo, *The Woman Who Fell From the Sky*.
8. Juan Felipe Herrera, *187 Reasons Mexicanos Can't Cross the Border: Undocuments 1971-2007*.
9. Russell Leong, *The Country of Dreams and Dust*.

10. Bob Kaufman, *Solitudes Crowded with Loneliness*.

11. Diane di Prima, *Revolutionary Letters*.

12. Jack Agüeros, *Sonnets from the Puerto Rican*.

13. Sesshu Foster, *City Terrace Field Manual*.

14. Amanda Ngoho Reavey, *Marilyn*.

15. Monica Ong, *Silent Anatomies*.

16. Mark Nowak, *Coal Mountain Elementary*.

17. Rajiv Mohabir, *The Cowherd's Son*.

18. Philip Metres, *Sand Opera*.

19. Carmen Giménez Smith, *Milk and Filth*.

20. Lisa Linn Kanae, *Sista Tongue*.

21. Alan Chong Lau, *Blues and Greens*.

22. Bruna Mori, *Dérive*.

Ask me in another ten years, and let's see what I have to say.

May 26, 2020 Letters to a Young Brown Girl and the brown girls who read this

What I wrote two years ago:

> *May 25, 2018: Manuscript progress, re: 'some brown girl.' It's looking more like "Letters to a Young Brown Girl."*

> *And I think folks who read it and get it will be the folks who understand why brown girls need to be reminded again and again and again that it is OK to speak your mind, that bravery is hard if not sometimes impossible, that this is a lifelong process of emerging from*

invisibility, of unlearning all the toxic self-erasing, all the spiritual self-harm that centuries of patriarchy have reinforced upon us.

That this lifelong process to undo these centuries of self-negation and policing, enforcing patriarchal rules is hard work many of us are afraid to do, and that many of us don't know where to start, if we ever even arrive at a place where we've chipped away at some small amount of that fear.

And those who don't know what I've just described above, those folks may read this work as repetitive and unnecessary.

I write this today, as *Letters to a Young Brown Girl* goes to print this month. It will be in my hands this summer. This is worth saying again and again; this is the kind of poetry I have always wanted to write, this music, and these long prose poems filled with details and images and language that is Pinay-specific, for Pinays before anyone else.

For brown girls who would know my range of emotions, as a brown girl raised in a culture that erases us and simultaneously demands our obedience and acquiescence.

For brown girls who rebel, who continue to rebel against norms that objectify and belittle us.

For brown girls who have been labeled "bad," exactly for that rebellion, against family tradition, against self-centered, misogynist boyfriends and romantic partners, and toxic social circles.

For brown girls who continue to rebel against white supremacism and internalized oppression.

For brown girls who have taken the weaponized gender and cultural expectations of white supremacism, and said, No, and said, Fuck You.

For brown girls who do not play nice for the convenience of others.

For brown girls who are afraid of the repercussions, who know this is a hard path, but who push, who rebel, who break free nonetheless. Even when their own community wants them to shut the hell up and be nice, they push, and they speak their minds, and they make art, and this art is the kind of art that saves you.

For the past few weeks, months, I have been witnessing on social media a number of young Pinxys asking for the kind of Filipino authored literature that interrogates, dismantles the María Clara archetype, that navigates kapwa and Filipino core values in this century, in diaspora, in this patriarchal and consumerist culture.

I am jumping out of my skin for this work to reach you.

June 16, 2020 The Book of Asking

Today I am having "trouble" writing another book. I am fighting with the book as a bound set of grand proclamations. How did I get here. That said, I am asking.

Questions while reading Pinay authored literature:

- What do we see, and what do we not see in the literature?
- What is women's work?
- Who gets to write books?
- Who has access to literacy?
- Who has access to formal education? To secondary education? To college education?
- Who has access to (constitutional and social) freedom of speech?
- What are the repercussions for speaking?
- Who has safe access to the outside world? Who has the power to leave the house?
- Who has time, energy, and space to write?
- Who has access to editors and publication? Who grants this access?
- Who has access to public platforms? Who grants this access?
- Who owns the means of literary production? How do they decide what is worthy of publication? What are their standards for determining what has literary merit?
- Who has access to the capital required to print and disseminate literature?
- What are the gendered, racialized, and socioeconomic realities of writing and publishing for women, immigrant women, women of color, third world women?
- What is acceptable for women to write about? Who determines what is acceptable?
- How can women, immigrant women, women of color, third world women resist? What are the repercussions of resistance?

Questions for Pinays Writing:

1. Who are your women ancestors, your women literary ancestors, role models? Who are the mythical and/or historical women figures informing your writing? How have they informed your writing? What have they taught you about how to write about women's lives, Pinay lives?

2. How do you write about the body, within the context of feminism, womanism, and/or Pinayism, about the Pinay body, as mother, as colonial (postcolonial, decolonizing) body. Given patriarchy, misogyny, given histories of imperialism, invasion, Christianization. Given diaspora, globalization, economics. Given popular culture. Given legislation. In other words, given the state of the Pinay body, the woman body in the world.

3. How did you find your voice? When did you find the courage to speak? What/who prevented you from speaking? What are the consequences of silence, and of choosing to break silence?

4. Regarding work, work ethic, "women's work," motherhood (if applicable, the decision to be a mother, the decision not to be a mother, or if motherhood is beyond your reach), what are your beliefs/thoughts on writing about domestic spaces and domestic work, about personal, private, intimate matters, especially given that such subject matter can be ghettoized as "women's writing."

5. Is your writing political? How specifically is it political? Why is it political, or why must it be political? For example, how are your aesthetic, linguistic, formalistic, genre choices deliberate, political choices as a writer who is a Pinay, a woman, a woman of color.

6. How do you navigate the American publishing industry as a woman of color, as a Pinay, especially when your subject matter may not be

on the radar or priority list of the mainstream. How do you navigate the publishing industry as a woman of color and Pinay, resisting objectification, resisting being tokenized or fetishized.

7. Given all of the above, what do we as writers say to future generations of Pinays, about voice, about self-determination, about the spaces we have fought for?

Communing With Redwoods on the California Coast

My summers for at least the past decade have found me and my husband
fleeing the illegal firework spectacles and screeching sideshows in
Oakland, Calif., and heading into the Santa Cruz mountains, down to
the Monterey Peninsula and across the iconic Bixby Bridge into Big Sur.
In coastal redwood groves I eavesdrop on children marveling at the oldest
of the trees. "It's so tall, it's as tall as the moon," one says to the other. I
think, "That line will end up in a poem I'll write soon." I can't help but
hug these giant trees and come away with my hair and arms covered in
spider webs; I thank them for sharing their space and whisper, "Excuse
us, we're just passing through."

Loggers cut down many of the eldest redwoods over a century ago, but
the trees' daughters grow in circles, or fairy rings, surrounding the
stumps, and fallen trunks are covered with moss and mushrooms —
turkey tail, pink-edge bonnet. We wonder what creatures or spirits
reside in the hollowed-out trunks. Along the almost dried-out creeks,
the blackberry bramble is thick and painful, but it offers the perfect
place to be still and spy on swallowtail butterflies. We climb uphill, the
terrain beneath the redwood canopies soft and cool, covered with
branches and needles. Their root systems sprawl and push up earth
into staircases. Still further uphill, we clear the tree line, and the
terrain is now fine white sand, what remains of an ancient ocean.
Redwoods have given way to fragrant sagebrush, to twisted, smooth red
bark manzanitas, to ponderosa pine, and we watch the woodpeckers
wage turf warfare upon one another.

On the Monterey Peninsula, we find sea otters floating on their backs in the kelp — off the coast of Pacific Grove and Point Lobos, and at the entrance to Moss Landing Harbor, where they roll their bodies around in the water, huffing and scrubbing their fur. We sit on the rocks and watch them, no more than two meters away from us, unbothered by our presence. On the other side of the breakwater, an otter dives into the surf and emerges with shellfish to crack open on its furry belly. The harbor seals are now pupping on the shores, and the salt air is filled with their barking. In the scrub of the Salinas River Beach dunes, we count the tiny brush rabbits darting into their burrows.

All of these things tell me something about poetry — observing life sprouting from fallen, burnt, dead things; the stillness and silence required to watch a single hummingbird drinking the nectar of monkey flowers; our smallness under the 200-foot-tall, thousand-year-old trees; spotting a kestrel or a Cooper's hawk hovering above us at the peak of a mountain. I think of that Gerard Manley Hopkins poem "The Windhover" — "the hurl and gliding / Rebuffed the big wind. My heart in hiding / Stirred for a bird … " As a lapsed (failed) Catholic — eight years at Holy Spirit School in Fremont, four years at Moreau Catholic High School in Hayward — I think, "My church is here, on the mountain, under the redwoods, by the sea."

~

When I was growing up in suburban Fremont, not too far from all this beauty, color and texture, I didn't know the names of trees, or flowers, or creatures. I'm sure I asked my parents, and I'm sure that they bought me and my sisters books, and took us to the public library as their way of telling us to look it up ourselves. The natural world was a faraway place, beyond what we could see from the car window on family road trips — to Cannery Row, to Hearst Castle, to Solvang and, ultimately, to Disneyland. Finding the trails leading up into the mountains, away from safe and tame tourist attractions, souvenir shops and public restrooms, was not something we did (I didn't know we could). How many painstakingly composed family photos do I have, of my three sisters, my parents, my cousins, my aunts and uncles, wearing clean white sneakers and clean bluejeans, cameras slung around our necks, American place names printed across our newly purchased T-shirts? I found so many of these photos in my grandfather's home in the small Philippine town of Gattaran, a harrowing 12-hour bus ride northeast of Manila. These were the keepsakes we sent "home," to show our large extended family what our "American" lives were like, our summers full of comfort, leisure and safety.

I would like to think my grandfather would recognize me now, not as the pristinely clothed teenager safely distanced from buzzing, crawling, skittering things but as his 50-year-old American granddaughter, emerging from the brush covered in sweat, burrs, bug bites, scratches and cuts from so much bramble, rocks in my socks and shoes, my legs coated with dust and mud, smelling like the sun, with a head full of poems waiting to be written down.

"The Rule is, Do Not Stop"

A Literary Address delivered for the Pilipinx American Library at the
Asian Art Museum, August 25, 2018

> You know what annoys me? People who won't see the through
> line from Joe Bataan to Bruno Mars. You ever wonder about
> the sound of a poet rappin' with ten thousand carabaos in the
> dark? You ever eat fish and rice with your hands, off styrofoam
> plates, in a hole in the wall, south of Market Street? You ever
> roll down your windows while speeding down Highway 101, to
> smell the Pajaro River? What if that's the poem, and you
> missed it, because you were looking for something roseate,
> effete, something that smells like prestige.

I'm Barbara Jane Reyes, and I am a poet. I say all of these things to you
today as a poet, one who works with line, lyric, and language — my
concerns and values are conveyed and contained in these. Something I
have been learning throughout the course of my formal and informal
education as a poet, is that we can and must make many spaces to tell
our stories in many different ways. These are the stories I tell.

When my parents immigrated here, they lived in a tiny apartment in
the Mission District. They soon moved to a tiny apartment in Daly
City. A couple of years later, they bought a home, and we moved to
Fremont. I grew up in Fremont. I went to kindergarten, and had eight
years of Catholic education in Fremont. I went to Catholic high school

in Hayward. I went to college in Berkeley. I went to grad school in San Francisco. I bought a home in Oakland. I am of here.

In Fremont, in the late 1970s, the tiny handful of other Filipinos that we knew were family friends, folks who knew my parents from way back. We called them cousins. In the 1970s, one of the priests at Holy Spirit Church was Filipino — Father Flores blessed our house. He also blessed my mother's brand new Toyota Celica. We lived by apricot orchards. It felt like outside of our family parties, no one knew what a Filipino was. I had no idea that our still agricultural Fremont, that California, that the West Coast, that Hawaii, were cultivated by thousands of Filipino laborers, who had been here for decades. If you return to Carlos Bulosan's *America is in the Heart*, see where Allos's train stops in empty grape fields in Niles. That's Fremont. He wakes up in San Jose. Fourth grade California History never mentioned us. American History mentioned the Philippine American War in passing, but did not say anything about our having come here. I never read anything a Filipino had written. How could I have possibly become an author under these conditions.

If I were to revisit Bulosan's "I am not a laughing man," I would see something of myself there, angry because no one ever told me or taught me that I could write what I could write, that it was not impossible, that it could have meaning larger than myself — the words I did not know I needed to commit to the page. No one ever told me that I could find my life in letters. Imagine that, the girl child of immigrants, an omission in literary and historical texts, thinking she could write books.

When I discovered I loved poetry, I didn't know that I had a right to. I didn't know poetry could ever be mine. Imagine, this scrappy little immigrant girl who was always ignored or shushed, who was always told to leave it and to do something more practical, who had come to believe that no one would ever be interested in the stories of her life and her family, who trekked to City Lights Books in North Beach and stayed for hours at a time, who dreamed she could one day have a place there. Who could imagine that.

I found Jessica Hagedorn's novel *Dogeaters* when I was 19. This was 1990. I learned that Hagedorn was once a scrappy young Filipina immigrant, who lived in San Francisco, who hung out at City Lights Books, who was mentored by Kenneth Rexroth. I learned that Hagedorn's first couple of collections of poetry — *Dangerous Music*, and *Pet Food & Tropical Apparitions* – were published by the indie publisher, Stephen Vincent's Momo's Press, here in San Francisco. I learned that Hagedorn was one of Ntozake Shange's colored girls in the choreopoem, *for colored girls who have considered suicide when the rainbow is enuf*. I learned, this is poetry.

I met Ray Orquiola in Professor Ronald Takaki's Asian American History class, in the Spring of 1990 at UC Berkeley. Ray told me he had just started *Maganda* magazine, and he was looking for young Filipino Americans to come and be a part of this thing. Imagine that; Filipino Americans publishing themselves and their own. Perhaps this is why I trusted him enough to hand him a stack of my handwritten poems in final versions, when only a few people very close to me had ever seen my poems.

I did my first poetry reading on April 29, 1990, for *Maganda* magazine, at the Faculty Glade on the UC Berkeley campus. We sat in the grass and I shared poems. This felt exactly how a poet should share poems, sitting in the grass on a lovely spring afternoon. There were perhaps seven or so people there, all Filipinos. My dad drove up from Fremont for this. His hay fever was so bad, he stood under a tree in the shade faraway but within eyesight. I don't know if he actually heard me speak. It would be easy to say, the rest is history. But let me say this instead: Publication enables your words to travel outside of yourself. It finds others like you, others who have been looking for someone like you. Because of *Maganda* magazine, I found Kearny Street Workshop and BAPAW. Or Kearny Street Workshop and BAPAW found me. That was the beginning of my public life in letters.

I found myself sharing the mic with Jaime Jacinto, with Jeff Tagami, with Shirley Ancheta, with Al Robles himself. Once, we read poetry in the Chinese Culture Center overlooking the hole in the ground on Kearny and Jackson Streets. It was like reading poetry to ghosts.

I wrote this poem in 2002. It's so old, I can't find an actual Word file of it; I suspect it's on one of the floppy disks I've held on to, though I have no computer that can read a floppy disk anymore.

ν

Placemarkers

For Al Robles, and for the Elders, whose stories he told

Kearny and Jackson, San Francisco, CA, Summer 2001: There's a
gaping hole in the ground in the middle of the overcrowded city; I've
never felt I'd earned the right to write about this gaping hole which you
gave a voice and face while all I could do was watch. I never thought it
was mine, the weeds and chunks of concrete and waste here. I can't
move from this spot; the breeze entangles my long hair into this chain
link fence now woven with my fingers. Ghosts I never knew, tricksters
and lovers, you should have just asked me to stay. I would've stayed.

Rizal Social Club, El Dorado and Lafayette, Stockton, CA, Autumn
2002: My hands flat upon these walls' cold leaden chips of white paint,
yellowed. Time could have forgotten, but now I can't take my palms
and forehead away from this coolness in Central Valley Sunday, where
elders in their finery shield their eyes, worked backbreaking fields until
they were unable, gathered here circa 1920, circa 1930, til it all closed
down. Down the street now, McDonald's; right behind us, a freeway.
Here I wish to keep my palms and bittersweetly baptized forehead on
this wall. I walk along its facade and the adjacent Mariposa Hotel. I
peer into its wrought iron gate to hear water drip, drip, upon cracked
concrete; I peer up through the rusted fire escape at the sky. I want to
see these slickly pomaded, sharp dressed spirits that I feel as I run my
palms along the crevices of walls; my fingers and love lines gather
ancient dirt and peeling paint. My brothers and sisters watch me
intently. They find no peculiarity in my attachment to a building I have
never seen before; they want to touch my hands for the dirt I have

collected. I have come here to be filled with you, you were here, all of you were here.

Saint Patrick's Church, 3rd Street and Mission, San Francisco, CA, Summer 1995: At an I-Hotel commemoration, cha-cha-ing in the church's basement, Rona and I are converged upon from opposite ends of the room by two Pinoys, one young, one old. The spiky haired frat boy in baggy blue jeans cuts in and moves with her, Northern Cali Style. I commit to memory the aftershave, the black fedora, the red silk tie patterned with black hearts, the red pressed silk shirt, the bone white blazer, the highly shined leather shoes of the old Pinoy who takes my hand as I immediately follow his dance steps. *Da rule is, do NOT stop,* waving the index finger of his left hand, he must be 80. I can't keep up with him.

Fillmore Street, San Francisco, CA: Jazz and life on the edges are daily improvisations when the streets are cold. Family is the folks who sit at your table, sell you the morning paper, wander this neighborhood and collect your stories for safekeeping. Poet Elder, you are conduit and vessel; your voice, a protest — who says history is only about dead white people! You have transcribed history: it's about us.

Dryden Road, Fremont, CA: Down the street from new Hong Kong money, a pho house, a parking lot filled with expensive SUVs and souped up rice rockets, I am of a different generation of suburban comfort in newly painted track homes. There once was an apricot orchard here; there once was a red farmhouse edged with white, a solitary oak tree and a hanging tire. Now my parents' house contains slick Japanese cars in a two-car garage. Jasmine vines and sunset colored hibiscus overrun the outer walls and trellises of their renovated home. Fragrance always drifts in through the open skylights. Manong, I feel you have been here before the dirt in my parents' backyard was always so fertile. The lemon tree is large as brushfire; its boughs hang low, heavy with fruit. I came here when degree professionals were in Cold War demand, when Martial Law tore our home apart. I never thought you would claim me as your little sister.

Clement Street, San Francisco, CA: Jaime always tells this story; when he was 15 years old walking through Chinatown, he met you, your hair out to here but a little less gray, your arms full of grocery bags. The star apples are what I remember most; the hermit Zen monk descending the mountain to nourish us. Inada says you were so Zen you didn't need to read your poetry, you just were. I have always wanted to write you poems; I just wanted you to remember my name, and when you did, I felt I had finally arrived.

ᶻ

I attended "Intimacy and Geography: The National Asian American Poetry Festival" in New York City in 2003. There, I met the Filipino American poets who would later go on to create Kundiman. They asked me over dinner, what was it like, the Filipino American poetry scene in San Francisco. I told them, it's deep, it's DIY, and lineage is everything — if Al Robles remembers who you are, then you have made it. Their eyes were so big in their faces. Who knows what they were thinking. How were they supposed to know what it meant, and how was it supposed to have any value to them. They were in and of a different world, one that at the time I wasn't so sure whether I could, whether I even wanted to be a part of. Back then, I felt, if I didn't adopt their definitions of success, one that from my vantage point, centered prestigious publishers and book awards, then I would always just be some scrappy brown girl from this far corner, this unruly margin of the country, and that wouldn't mean anything to this body called American Poetry.

I never wanted my writing education to take me away from this place, and from this community. I wanted my writing education to make me stronger at writing about my, our being here. I was the only Pinay in my poetry program at San Francisco State. Imagine that. Where roughly 2000 students in the entire student body identify as Filipino. In the Bay Area, where over 450,000 Filipinos live. Those odds could stop a Pinay, erase a Pinay, silence her before she's even learned she has a voice.

But there are so many of us, Pinay and Pinoy writers and artists, aggressively, courageously creating bodies of evidence, even master works, of our being here, living and breathing and struggling here. We've been here. We're still here.

Not alien, we are of here.
Not alien, *have come, am here* –

Among the xenophobes,
The deadbeat dads and gangstas

Among the white liberals,
People who mind colored folks

Among the dirty hipsters,
Over-schooled armchair activists

Among the sex traffickers,
White supremacists, wife beaters

Among the day laborers,
Undocumented dreamers

Among the inalienable,
The PTSDed, the evicted

Among the emigrated,
The refugees, the polyglots

Among the accented Taglish
Speaking, *have come, am here.*

In this fast and gritty place, we are creating spaces for us to congregate, to explore and hone our craft, to amplify. We are defining our own literary and artistic traditions. We are not asking for anyone's permission.

I write here, in this place my family and I have found and made our lives. I write to discover the complexity of our lives in this place. In poetic lines, the details of our lives reveal themselves, and here, we make meaning. When we buried my father here, I wrote like hell; that was all I could do.

ર

The Day

two fingers on a pulse like the true point – Angela Narciso Torres
gloss of feathers dimmed in the orange quiescence of the sun – Lehua Taitano
a damaged beauty, a music I can't manage, no words – Urayoán Noel

645 am. The very last meal I had with my father was arroz negro y petrale
sole paella, fideua caldosa, pork bellies, okra, and a bourbon elderflower
cocktail, in Uptown Oakland at Duende. Four days later, his brain got
lost in language. *No words.* His body forgot how to walk and how to
swallow. His lungs decided to stop taking air. He never came home. He is
on my mind when I go to sleep. He is on my mind when I wake up.

836 am. At the AC Transit 26 bus stop, I am late to my day job.
Morning commute reminds me of my father, coconut oil slicked hair
behind his ears, duck tail in the back. He ironed the creases in his
slacks. He left the house with Ralph Lauren Polo aftershave on his
collar. He clipped his Bechtel badge to his pocket protector. Protractor,
mechanical pencils, drafting tools arranged within reach, thermos of
coffee in his DYMO labeled briefcase, ten-speed bike to Union City
BART station. That was before coconut oil became trendy. That was
before the layoffs and unemployment checks. After this, combing his
hair became a chore.

902 am. Lehua told me that daughters stolen from their homelands do
not lose their power. Their tongues, their palates adapt. New roots and
unbloomed buds – bullets – become new spells, new medicine. You do
not get lost on an island. You take pieces of it – shell, sand, seed – with

you when you must take flight. Jelly jars, perfume vials, Tupperware, Ziploc bags, use what you've got.

1021 am. This is when I learned that if you present at the pharmacy early to purchase your DEA-regulated allotment of pseudophedrine, the pharmacy staff will eye you, speak to you like you are a meth head and a fucking criminal. #FML

1050 am. "Izabel Laxamana, a 13-year-old girl in Tacoma, Washington died by suicide after jumping off a highway overpass on Friday, May 29. Days before, Laxamana's father ... had reportedly punished her for an unspecified transgression by cutting off her hair and uploading a video to YouTube."

1127 am. I belong in this fluorescent-lit cubicle. The privilege of the fluorescent-lit cubicle, where I thumb through thousand-page, spiral-bound indexes. According to the International Classification of Diseases (ICD-10-CM), F43.20, Adjustment Disorder, Unspecified, includes culture shock, grief reaction, and nostalgia. To be a Pinay daughter is classifiable, diagnosable, reimbursable with the proper documentation. It is a disorder. It requires professional intervention. It may require a prescription. To be a Pinay daughter may be covered by your managed care plan. To be a Pinay daughter should be covered by Obamacare. Please consult your manual.

1153 am. Filipino writers on social media asking me why I must write about Filipino things. Don't I fear being seen only as a Filipino writer. Won't I just write about normal things, universal human truths, love and whatnot. Won't I read the important books they say they intend to write. For sake of bayanihan, won't I hook up a fellow Filipino, introduce them to my non-Filipino publishers.

1214 pm. There are ladybugs on my father's grave.

220 pm. You're all girls? You don't have any brothers? Your poor father. How awful that must have been for him. Your mother never gave him any sons.

222 pm. My sisters and I all kept our father's name.

303 pm. I must tell you that the first time I heard Prince's "Controversy," was on KDIA 1310 am in 1981. I was 10, dancing and tingling. I'd never heard anything like this, falsetto, synth, electric guitar, and liminality. Because of KDIA, I know that the following year, The Gap Band dropped *Gap Band IV*. My older sister owned it on vinyl, 33-⅓, gatefold LP. It is a perfect album. Let no one tell you different.

432 pm. I am tired of talking about talking about race. These are the facts: I was born on the same island where my mother was born, where my father was born. Where my mother's mother, and my mother's father, where my father's mother, and my father's father were born. Go back many more generations, and you will find our birthplaces are that very same island. *The true point* should not be why I write this, but how, in whose tongues.

435 pm. You do not get lost on an island.

502 pm. *Two fingers on a pulse.* He was still, breathing when I left his room. He was, and one by one they were wheeling away machines. The blipping monitor told me what my hands felt still. He was warm. He was 73. He was a tough motherfucker, stubborn enough to live to 100, so that he could grumble and elbow us, so that he could give us mad side eye. Instead, just hum and blip. Hum and blip. *A music I can't manage.* Exhale. *No words.*

524 pm. Sometimes you are damaged. You think poetry will repair you. You think poetry should repair you. You shake your fist at it when it doesn't. You walk hand-in-hand with your damage, into the world. You do not speak. You are surprised when people register you are there.

551 pm. Sometimes I can snap out of invisibility. On 8th and Broadway, Marshawn Lynch and I make eye contact. I refrain from telling him that it's my birthday, and may I please take a selfie with him. Why can't this interaction have happened with Draymond Green instead. #oaktown #DubNation

621 pm. There is no printed news story I can find about Norife Herrera Jones, that does not emphasize her dismemberment, and the esteemed alma mater of her estranged 74-year old white husband, her murderer.

753 pm. You don't have kids? Why don't you have kids? You should have kids. How terrible it must be for your husband. You should give your husband kids. You are a bad wife. How terrible it must be for your parents. You should give your parents grandkids. You are a bad daughter.

802 pm. Think Tatsuya Nakadai in *Harakiri*, unleashing his no fucks left to give, one man wrecking machine on an entire estate of samurai turned peacetime paper pushers. Dying of boredom and leisure time. The rōnin Nakadai thrusting his katana through hollow armour, keeping it real.

903 pm. *On a pulse* that stopped. The breathing stopped. He was warm, but the breathing stopped. Now he *flies to greet my ancestors, gloss of feathers dimmed in the orange quiescence of the sun there is no need now* for sublingual drops of morphine, for the sleep that let him slip away from us.

905 pm. *I can't manage, no words.*

911 pm. Sometimes you are broken. Poetry won't fix you. Poetry can't fix you. It doesn't have lungs to give you its air. It doesn't have hands to stitch your parts back together. To make you tea. To drive you home.

949 pm. Death row prisoner and human trafficking victim Mary Jane Veloso celebrates women's rights with a prison fashion show. Veloso has just modeled a sheer, embroidered sheath dress at Wirogunan Prison. On death row. Curlicues and up-do, perfect eyebrows and pearl manicure. Always a breath away from the firing squad.

1026 pm. My #WCW Pia Alonzo Wurtzbach's Instagram tells me that she has just learned the proper mechanics of the fast ball. Noah Syndergaard taught her this, for Filipino Heritage Night at Citi Field. In my perfect world, Pia would throw out the first pitch at AT+T Park. Tim Lincecum would still be our ace. He would be the one to teach her how to throw, even though Timmy's "The Freak." Arnel Pineda would sing, "Lights," in the middle of the eighth. All the starstruck Filipinos in the house would radiate so much light, we'd be the fucking Maharlika Nebula Supernova of San Francisco.

11:55 pm. I remember holding the dove's warmth in my palms. I was still, it was still, it was waiting for me to unlace my fingers. There, the horizon above a young oak tree, mustard flowers, poppies, and autumn snails, the dove's gentle bones pushed off my palms, into *the orange quiescence of the sun*. This is how I said good-bye to my father — shouting his name at the sky.

11:57 pm. I sometimes remember to floss. I always wear socks to bed, even in the summertime. I sometimes build a pillow fort. I always think about that day. That with my mother's permission, they wheeled my father out of the hospital covered in a velvet shroud. That I could not sleep for a long time. That I would not close my eyes. That every night noise might have been him visiting me.

ᴈ

I'm an elder now, yes? Grieving has made me go gray. I've been at this for decades. Poets have come up with me. Arlene Biala, Tony Robles. Poets continue coming up. Aimee Suzara, Janice Sapigao, Rachelle Cruz, Jason Bayani. In the South Bay, in the suburbs, in Oakland, in San Francisco. We're not stopping anytime soon. We're pushing. There will always be a 19 year old Pinay who comes through my classroom, a young Pinay who finds our books and feels a little less invisible, who feels emboldened to commit her words to the page, who feels emboldened to tell her own stories. I write here, grounded in the world and the community which has nurtured and sustained me and challenged me, the very writers and authors who first said to me, "We see you, sister. We see you, and we got you."

Pakikipagkapwa-tao

Hella indigenous, which does not mean gone native. Kakayahan umunawa sa damdamin ng iba, for real. You know, like Ruby Ibarra and one hundred Pinays giving you resting bitch face. You know, like those syndicated, full color photographs, of boys and men in LeBron James and Steph Curry jerseys, thinned flipflops on their feet, one body together, shouldering a nation. One bamboo hut at a time. One set of lungs breathing. One heart. Isang mahal. Isang bagsak.

Acknowledgments

"Is this Diasporic Pinay Mythopoetics" is an edited version of my response to Christina Newhard's questions for "Creatures of Midnight: Six Philippine Mythmakers on Their Work."

"On Being an Immigrant Poet" first appeared in the anthology, *Others Will Enter the Gates: Immigrant Poets on Poetry, Influences, and Writing in America* (Black Lawrence Press, 2015).

"To Decenter English" first appeared in the anthology, *American Poets in the 21st Century: Poetics of Social Engagement* (Wesleyan University Press, 2018).

"What's This Thing About Orientals Together On A Bus," first appeared as a Literary Address on the Smithsonian Asian Pacific American Center website.

"What Does It Mean to be an APIA Author 'In These Times'," first appeared in *Kartika Review*, Issue 17 (Spring 2017).

"Communing With Redwoods on the California Coast" first appeared in *The New York Times T Magazine* (July 22, 2021).

"The Rule is, Do Not Stop" was delivered as a Literary Address for the Pilipinx American Library at the Asian Art Museum on August 25, 2018.

BARBARA JANE REYES is a longtime Bay Area poet, author, and educator. She is the author of *Letters to a Young Brown Girl* (BOA Editions, Ltd., 2020), *Invocation to Daughters* (City Lights Publishers, 2017), *To Love as Aswang* (Philippine American Writers and Artists, Inc., 2015), *Diwata* (BOA Editions, Ltd., 2010), *Poeta en San Francisco* (TinFish Press, 2005), and *Gravities of Center* (Arkipelago Books Publishing, 2003). She teaches Pinay Literature, and Diasporic Filipina/o/x Literature in the Yuchengco Philippine Studies Program at the University of San Francisco. She lives with her husband, poet and educator Oscar Bermeo, in Oakland.